THE PRINCIPLES OF
PUBLIC PERSONNEL ADMINISTRATION

THE PRINCIPLES OF PUBLIC PERSONNEL ADMINISTRATION

by

Fred Telford

Edited by
Charles P. Messick
with
William W. Boyer

UNIVERSITY OF DELAWARE
NEWARK, DELAWARE

Contents:

CONTENTS

Foreword

Personnel managers and practitioners of today—perhaps because of the press of their day-to-day responsibilities—have little interest or understanding of the problems and difficulties of those of us, their predecessors, who developed the perspectives and procedures of modern personnel management. While they follow and incorporate those practices in their effective actions today—often as unquestioned postulates—we and they are far from realizing that government is no better than those who do its work and direct its affairs, a truism too often overlooked.

I have learned many things from my own early experience in personnel management that one may not find in textbooks. Although I waited too long to reduce some of these things to writing, finally I published an account of what seem to me important points or processes in my actions that have been favorably received over the years.*

For half a century, Fred Telford was one of my associates. To my knowledge, he had one of the most extensive and intensive careers in personnel administration to this date. He was right there on the firing line where people were at work, decisions were made and directions were given. He was a man who acted on his own ideas and wrote down his own results and conclusions. One of the very few students and administrators of personnel of his day who sensed the proportions and the significance of the fledgling

*Charles P. Messick, *An Adventure in Public Personnel Administration* (University of Delaware, Newark, Delaware 1973).

field of personnel administration, his weakness, although it is hardly fair to designate it as such, was that he was always in a hurry. He always wanted to find the answer to the problem at hand and move on to the next.

I first met and became associated with Telford in 1917 and as early as 1925 I asked him to prepare this book and a series of manuals. He did begin work on this book and some of the manuals at that time, but his work always came first and when he found the time to write this book his health had failed. The manuscript is thus incomplete in some instances. After his death, I undertook to do some editing and rewriting where necessary to prepare the manuscript for publication. While the passing of time has made some of the material obsolete, I feel strongly that the precepts that Telford developed in those early days of personnel management are as sound now as they were then. The tools hammered out then have been tried in the field and have been found to still apply.

Fred Telford came into his life's work by chance. Born in 1884 on a farm near Cairo, Illinois, he always excelled in school and eventually went on to Southern Illinois Teachers Training College, where he became an instructor even before his graduation. Following his graduation he went to Alaska as a teacher for several years, returning to Chicago to marry and start to raise his family. He and his wife wrote for local magazines and by chance he drifted into writing for a civil service publication. This led to his introduction to H.O. Griffenhagen who had been employed by the Chicago Park System to organize its civil service employees into working units. It was Griffenhagen who first developed the tool of job "classification," a concept Telford discusses in depth in this book. After forming Griffenhagen and Associates, the group was engaged by the Canadian government in 1918 to make a thorough study of all of the Dominion Government's departments and agencies, including personnel. This was the largest such project undertaken anywhere in the world up to that time. Telford had joined Griffenhagen's organization in 1917 and soon became the top assistant in that work with the Canadian government. I myself worked for a time with them on that study and it was there I first became associated with Telford.

Telford was instrumental in the success of the Canadian study. Building up Griffenhagen's concept of job classification,

Telford added first an extended definition in a statement of the kind of work to be done by the incumbent of each position and, in a further step, he added examples of work. As a final step to the class description', the qualification—education and experience— or the alternatives for each were added. Thus Telford created the full class specifications. Changes in wording and arrangement of items involved have been and are yet being made, but the base class descriptions made then are yet sound and are still accepted and used. Following this study, the U.S. government engaged Griffenhagen and Associates to do a similar but less extensive study. Telford was active in this study also. But whereas the Canadian government accepted the results of the study and put the findings to use, the U.S. government allowed the results to quietly become forgotten.

Impressed by Telford's ability and experience, I brought about his appointment as director of the Bureau of Public Personnel Administration, which I had organized in 1922. During the ten years in which the Bureau functioned (1922-1932) Telford was its director. The real foundations of a positive merit system were shown to be possible and its place and part in public administration were established and proved during this period. Telford played a major part in my efforts to turn personnel agencies from negative organizations, outside the general administration of government or business, to positive bodies with a major part to play in the organization.

While I was demonstrating the place and the part of constructive personnel administration in New Jersey, and its possibilities in relation to effective and economical government, Mr. Telford was travelling up and down and across the United States and Canada inspecting, aiding, encouraging, teaching and challenging personnel management administrators, departmental authorities, and all who would listen, about these accruing advantages. And he reported the conditions he found to all those who read the Bureau's monthly magazine, *Public Personnel Studies*. Telford supervised and directed the publication of this magazine and wrote much of its contents. He served in these capacities for the life of the Bureau which were the halcyon days of personnel management in America. When the effects of the depression of 1929 were felt, the Bureau was obliged in 1932 to discontinue its operations for the time being. Telford then entered the national services as a member of a group studying the problems of finding suitable applicants for air force pilots and methods of training them. While the records of that project are tied up in the volumes of our national defense records, it is known that Telford was again successful in his efforts as a leader in that project.

I continually urged Telford to work on this manuscript, feeling then, as I do now, that it is needed to fill an important gap in the history of the development of the science, if such it be, and the art of personnel management. I asked him to write from the position of knowing about—not only hearing or reading about—personnel management. He began writing a book entitled "The Principles of Personnel Management," but by reason of the other work he was trying to do for the Bureau he was unable to complete the task. After the Second World War, with the exception of his association with me when I carried on a consulting service, he resumed his writing. Ultimately, he completed a voluminous and repititious manuscript as well as two or three other works, none of which were in publishable form.

Because I have long known that a written treatise—a basic book covering the field of public personnel management—was needed to fill in the history of the upward march of the recognized value of the personnel story, I—with the approval of Telford's daughters and the urging of many of my former associates—have undertaken to rewrite these "principles" in the hope that the personnel story will not only be completed but these "principles" may prove helpful to those who come after me.

This book is a serious effort to set down in a kind of logical order the precepts of personnel administration. What is to be found here is not new and parts have been tried in many places, but it is safe to say that no one in personnel management has heretofore undertaken to put into effect the well-balanced administration described by Telford. Since there are many words, terms and phrases that mean the same thing, Telford's extensive list of definitions has been made into a glossary and placed at the end of the book for easy reference.

Telford's edited work should serve as a reference textbook and guide for administrators, technicians, educators, and students by one of its ablest advocates and practitioners. For this reason, and for reasons of personal friendship, I have been happy to edit and aid in the publication of this book.

I must add to the foregoing comments that I am deeply appreciative for the help I have received in this rewriting from Dr. William W. Boyer, Charles P. Messick Professor of Public Administration at the University of Delaware, and from Judith H. Kidd, his able and experienced editorial assistant. In my advancing years, no longer have I had the endurance or skill to undertake this task alone. Without their help, so willingly given, this book would not have been completed.

We have tried to write as nearly as possible in Mr. Telford's own style. We have failed in this effort in many parts, of course. We have tried, however, to tell the story as it has developed. We hope it will find its place in the public personnel records of America and be helpful to others.

CHARLES P. MESSICK
Rehoboth, Delaware
January 1976

Introduction and Acknowledgements

Putting into book form an extensive body of knowledge is always an ambitious undertaking. When the subject matter deals with a relatively new and rapidly developing science and art, it is a major project to prepare a statement that will be at once adequate, well-organized, accurate, enlightening, and as far as possible objective. Two factors have led me to attempt this: the first is the urging of Charles P. Messick and others; the second is that throughout the fifty years this particular science and art have been developing, I have worked in the field. I believe I have had better opportunity than any other person to participate in the varied types of personnel work, to circulate, to observe, to experiment, to discuss problems with numerous personnel practitioners, and to note and appraise personnel successes and failures. While it is impossible to record all of the significant factual information or to state in final form the conclusions to be drawn from such information, I feel confident that I can provide a sound foundation as a guide for the work of others.

I have had in mind a number of groups who could profit from this book. At the top of that list are the numerous personnel practitioners who must, day by day, cope with personnel problems without the opportunity I had to travel all over the country over a long period of time, noting how others dealt with similar problems. Second on my list of those who might benefit are the able and ambitious young people who, usually at the college level, are preparing to become personnel technicians; third, there are those who have the task of guiding and assisting such young people who are yet in school or college through classroom work. I have had in mind, fourth, those legislative, executive, administrative, and operating officers who have to make personnel decisions and the officers and employees affected by such decisions. They may desire to inform themselves, at least broadly, about just what is involved in establishing and administering a sound personnel system. And, finally, I believe that this book will be helpful for those who, out of sheer curiosity or because of their desire to be informed citizens, wish to gain some insight into the more significant conceptions, principles, operations, and procedures involved in establishing, maintaining, changing, and discontinuing employer-employee relationships.

While I have had a modest part in helping to make the science and the art of personnel management what they have become, my purpose in preparing this book has not been to paint the personnel picture that I would like to see. Instead it has been to tell the story of what has happened in the personnel field, to indicate where we now stand, and to point out the direction in which we are now headed. It is impossible, of course, in one volume, to present and explain all the significant facts and conclusions involved but I have sought to present and explain those that seem to me most meaningful. I have tried, too, to express the conclusions that the more active and more successful practitioners as a group have reached; I have tried very hard not to substitute my own conclusions for those of this group.

I would like to acknowledge all those who, at various times in the past fifty years, have patiently explained and shown to me their personnel work and who have answered the hundreds of questions I have put to them. More than two hundred persons—mainly personnel practitioners but also educators, psychologists, statisticians, representatives of professional, trade, civic, and business groups, and legislative, executive, and administrative officers—have assisted me in various ways to gain such insight I have as to personnel operations and their meaning. They are too numerous to mention, but there are four people who have assisted directly and materially in the selection, organization, and presentation of the material contained in this book. They are Charles P.

Messick, formerly the executive officer of the State Department of Personnel of New Jersey, president of the Civil Service Assembly of the United States and Canada (now the International Personnel Management Association), and member of the governing body of the Bureau of Public Personnel Administration; William Brownrigg, who has served as the executive head of the central personnel agencies of the states of California and Michigan and the United States Department of Justice; and Robert J. Lacklen and Allen O. Gamble, personnel director and assistant personnel director of the National Aeronautics and Space Administration.

FRED TELFORD
Washington, D.C.
July 1, 1961

PART I

PRINCIPLES OF PERSONNEL MANAGEMENT

Introduction to Part I

Not many of us—even those whose business it is to devote their time and effort to personnel management—always keep in mind that there are a number of situations in personnel administration that keep occurring and recurring. The mathematician is inclined to call the rules describing or dealing with these events theorems, but this term connotes a precision and certainty that cannot be guaranteed in a field dealing with people. Knowledge has not yet reached a point where the actions and reactions of people can be systematically controlled and predicted. The word "factors" has been selected as the one that best describes the separate elements of the foundation of the personnel management field.

If the factors discussed in this section of the book are essentially correct, then the framework within which personnel management operations must be carried on becomes reasonably clear. The framework covers tangible and intangible elements and takes cognizance of numerous participants of many types and levels in personnel operations. It recognizes the complex relationships among these participants. It includes a large number of personnel management working procedures that are yet unfamiliar even to many of those directly or indirectly affected. It includes the development and use of varied types of transactions that occur and recur in establishing, maintaining, changing and discontinuing the employer-employee relationship.

The personnel management factors to be discussed are so important to the study of the field of personnel administration that Part I of this book is devoted to a discussion of them. While not all practitioners and people experienced in personnel administration would agree with the grouping and the stating of them, all would probably agree that these factors do exist and that by putting them into usable categories phenomena otherwise perplexing can begin to achieve some order and reason.

CHAPTER 1

Recognition of and Responsibility for Handling Personnel Transactions

Every employer and every employee must become aware, at least for a short time, of the existence of the first personnel management factor. In any organization having one or more employees, personnel transactions inevitably occur and recur in establishing, maintaining, changing and discontinuing the employer-employee relationship. They become aware, too, that these personnel transactions must be formally or informally attended to. The potential employer and the potential employee must, when they are considering the establishment of the employer-employee relationship, meet to discuss and consider such matters as the rate of pay, the qualifications needed, the qualifications possessed by the applicant, the hours and conditions of work, and the length of the term of employment. When the employer-employee relationship has been established, they then find another area of mutual interests and concerns. The employee must be provided with work space, supplied with tools and other equipment, given his first work assignment, and informed of or shown the work standards that he is expected to meet. Later they collaborate when annual or sick leave is to be taken, when payments for services performed are made, when there are changes in the work assignment, and when the employment of the employee is to be discontinued. If all goes well, the employer (directly or through his authorized agent) and the employee collaborate in the handling of those personnel transactions that affect them both, but it may come about eventually that they find themselves disagreeing to such an extent that there is a suspension, a resignation, a discharge, a lockout, or a strike.

Roles in Personnel Transactions

For the most part neither the employer nor the employee thinks of these personnel transactions as occurrences that make up a part of the personnel management operations of the organization. Neither is likely to use the term "personnel transaction" in communicating with the other. But each, from time to time, becomes keenly aware that the events I call personnel transactions actually do take place. The whole working force and employing force in this country constitute more than half of our total population. They are directly affected by or are actively participating in the personnel transactions that occur and recur in establishing, maintaining, changing, and discontinuing the employer-employee relationship. That they tend to be unaware of their exact roles in the personnel management operations involved does not change the fact that they do have such roles.

Some of the personnel management activities involved in establishing, maintaining, changing, and discontinuing the employer-employee relationship are made simpler or more complex by the activities of an intermediary. In many occupations and establishments, for example, the employee joins an appropriate union or he accepts the rate of pay and the work conditions upon which the employer and the union may already have agreed. If a strike is called, the employee must participate; if there is a lockout, he suffers the consequences.

In different organizations there are many variations in the procedures for handling personnel transactions. If a specific employer has but a few employees, he may rely upon his memory to store the significant facts when a specific personnel transaction occurs. The large employer, however, cannot depend upon memory. He must have many personnel records and he must, if he is to achieve desired personnel objectives consistently, adopt personnel procedures, put them in writing, and make them known to his employees and especially to those who participate in handling

4

personnel transactions. In large organizations, moreover, the employer must devise, adopt, and use a number of carefully contrived and designed personnel tools, including a position classification plan, a pay plan, a recruiting plan, an employee rating plan, a leave plan, and a separation plan to achieve any high degree of consistency in the personnel actions taken.

In this book most attention is given to the employer-employee relationship and to the personnel transactions involved in large organizations of two or three thousand positions or more. Particular attention is given to the occurrence and handling of personnel transactions in large government organizations because these are the ones that have taken the lead in developing and using the science and the art of personnel management. This does not alter the fact that personnel transactions occur and recur and must be attended to in any organization. There is no choice, even in the very small organization, about whether both the employer and the employee will or will not have a part in these relationships; this is guaranteed by the nature of human relationships in employment matters. The choice we do have is between the disregard of the personnel transactions as such and their conscious and considered recognition; between personnel order and disorder; between personnel improvisations and carefully considered procedures; between consistent and inconsistent personnel actions; and between the regular attainment of predetermined personnel objectives and failure.

Responsibility for Personnel Transactions

Basically, the recognized personnel management operations of any organization are handled, finally determined, and then implemented by the managing officers and by their authorized agents. This conception leaves out the personnel activities and the personnel pressures of various interested "outside" individuals and groups attempting to gain their own ends. These "outside" groups may include labor organizations, trade and professional organizations, civic and business organizations, political parties (as distinguished from the elective officers), and individuals who are intellectually, economically, or politically influential. This conception also leaves out the personnel activities of the officers and employees of the organization, except as they participate in the handling of personnel transactions and the development of various personnel tools.

Without some such limitations concerning the responsibility for the personnel management operations, however, widespread personnel confusion almost surely ensues. When the employer-employee relationship is being established, for example, there is likely to be a divergence in their pay objectives. The problems involved in establishing the beginning rate of pay can be approached from the viewpoint of either the potential employee or the potential employer. But there can be little doubt that, when analyzing personnel matters, the more reasonable approach is to look at them from the position of the managing officers of the organization and of their authorized agents, since they know of the financial matters involved and have the authority to handle the personnel transactions, make the formal and final personnel decisions, and implement whatever final personnel decisions are made.

This does not and should not mean that the employer, in handling the personnel transactions and in making and implementing the personnel decisions, will disregard the hopes of his employees, or that he will pay no attention to the objectives, desires, and demands of the interested "outside" groups and individuals. The effective employer, before he decides upon some proposed personnel action, does try to weigh and consider the attitudes and desires of those who will be directly affected by the action taken. He also considers the attitudes and possible actions of the interested "outside" groups and individuals. But however strong the inside and "outside" influences and pressures may be, it is still the employer who has the authority, who formally makes the personnel decisions, and who must implement them.

It is for these reasons that the authority of the managing officers and their authorized agents in personnel operations is accepted as valid. All the following discussions are based upon the conclusion that the personnel management operations in any organization should be regarded as those handled, finally decided upon, and then implemented by the managing officers of the organization and their authorized agents.

CHAPTER 2

The Influence and Role of Interested "Outside" Individuals or Groups on Personnel Management Operations

It must always be kept in mind that personnel management operations are not done in a vacuum. In our complex society, all of us are influenced by others—by friends, by fellow-workers, by government and business, by the mores of our times.

Some of these "outside" influences in the personnel and other fields are well known. Those who broadcast radio and television programs take account of the times of the day, the week, and the year when those of varying ages, interests, and tastes are free to look and listen. The distributors of household foods take into account prices, packaging, and deliveries. The home builder has due regard for seasons, current housing fashions and demands, and prices. All of us must pay attention to legal requirements and limitations. Similarly, the personnel management planner, designer, and practitioner must give due weight to the expectations, desires, and demands of "outsiders" who interest themselves in this or that phase of his personnel management operations.

These interested outside individuals or groups include the employee groups, usually acting through designated representatives; the trade or professional groups made up of workers in a given trade or profession who have as their principal aim the recognition, education, social and economic betterment, and entertainment of their members; the civic groups organized

7

primarily to help bring about the improvement of social or economic conditions and relations; the business groups organized primarily to help bring about the improvement of business conditions and relations; the taxpayer and stockholder groups organized primarily to influence the actions of governments or businesses; the political organizations, in and out of power, that seek to control and operate our national, state, and local governments; and the members of the press who report personnel management activities of interest to their readers. Of these groups, only those made up of operating employees have as their principal aim the influencing of personnel management operations. The others are often more concerned with what goes on in other fields than they are with personnel management operations.

Role of Employee Groups

The employee groups, naturally, have the greatest influence of any of these groups upon personnel management operations. Such groups are of many types and sizes, with major and minor variations in their personnel management aims. Some groups at times actively cooperate in the establishment and administration of an effective and comprehensive personnel management system in their respective organizations. Cooperation takes such forms as assisting in obtaining needed personnel management legislation; obtaining appropriation of funds for the central personnel agency; development, adoption, and revision of the classification and pay plans; carrying on recruiting operations; and facilitating the communications among managing officers, staff of the central personnel agency, and employees. The temptation to seek an advantage or benefit when the circumstances are propitious is sometimes irresistible, but very seldom in the public service does any employee group seek the scuttling or abandonment of whatever personnel management system has been built up over the years in its organization.

Few of the employee groups made up wholly or mostly of workers in business organizations seek to attain their objectives by aiding in building up sound and comprehensive personnel management systems in those organizations. They quite generally seek their own ends by means of persuasion, bargaining, organized action, strikes, boycotts, slowdowns, and even physical force. In many business organizations they have taken over a large share of the personnel management functions. The managing officers in the business organizations concerned, once dominant and dictatorial themselves in the handling of personnel manage- ment operations, now at times resist the personnel management demands of the organized employee groups. In the main they are loath to give up the broad personnel objective most generally sought by the managing officers of both government and business organizations—a personnel well qualified, well but not extrava- gantly paid, and so utilized as to be highly productive and therefore as small as possible in number.

Other Interest Groups

The trade and professional groups differ from employee groups in that their personnel management objectives are dis- tinctly subordinate to their other aims. These groups include clerical, nursing, engineering, accounting, medical, psychological, agricultural, and numerous other "associations," "assemblies," and "institutes." These groups often seek the recognition and consistent use of their trade and professional practices, standards, and nomenclature when a position classification plan is being developed or revamped. They often have "professional" stan- dards that they ask to be governing when qualifications are specified by the classification and recruiting technicians. As a rule the trade and professional groups willingly and helpfully collabo- rate in recruiting operations when allowed to do so. And they quite generally aid the pay technicians in determining what constitutes equity among the varied trade and occupational groups when the rates and scales of pay are being worked out.

The civic groups—neighborhood organizations, women's groups, bureaus of municipal research, civil service reform as- sociations, and the like—are, to the extent their interest extends to personnel management matters, likely to concern themselves with public rather than business personnel activities. They often stimulate the legislative body and the chief executive to develop, adopt, and implement the local, state or national personnel management programs. The bureaus of municipal research and similar groups are, as a rule, at their very best when the administrative personnel management operating work is being done. They not only observe, analyze, and appraise, but often actively participate in what is going on. They may stimulate the revision of the classification, pay, recruiting, employee rating, retirement, and other plans; in some cases, they actually take over part of the development, installation, and early administrative work.

The actual role of the political organizations in personnel management operations is little understood. Wide publicity is given to the actions that are reprehensible in seeking appointments of party members to positions in the public service for which they are not qualified, and their protection in office of these appointees, or other questionable procedures with contracts and bids. But their continuous part in the carrying on of essential personnel management work and their constructive actions in bringing about the authorization, establishment, and effective administration of sound and comprehensive personnel management systems in public jurisdictions are rarely recognized.

It was the Congress that accepted and enacted the initial civil service act for portions of the civil service of the national government of the United States submitted by civil service reformers following the assassination of President Garfield. It was the Congress, not the President nor the reformer, which in1917, 1918, 1919, and 1920, concerned itself with remedying the all but intolerable personnel management conditions in the national civil service of the United States produced by World War I. It was the legislature, politically controlled, that quickly enacted the needed personnel legislation when the Governor set out to put in order the personnel house in Maryland. No new classification plan, no new pay plan, no new recruiting plan has much chance of acceptance and implementation unless the political party in power gives it at least passive support; many times it acts positively and with considerable understanding of what is involved when the crucial decisions are made.

Finally, the representatives of the press have more than a lowly part in personnel management. Without question their role is more significant in the public service than in business organizations. Primarily the press representatives busy themselves with at least four types of personnel events: changes in personnel management legislation, policies and rules; changes in the higher officers; changes in the manner of handling personnel management operations; and personnel management scandals and irregularities. Also, when significant information about recruiting or classification plans or proposed actions is called to their attention, they are likely to be the main source of public information.

All of these individuals and groups have influence on the managing officers of an organization and roles to play when personnel management operations are considered and carried out.

CHAPTER 3

Personnel Objectives and Tools

There is no ready answer for every personnel emergency, or even for many of the recurring personnel problems. They are human problems and cannot be totally predicted and prepared for. But to assure as far as possible the effective handling of personnel management problems, the managing officers must determine, state with considerable definiteness, and make known to those in the organization just what personnel objectives are to be sought when the personnel management operations are taken care of. Having done this, the appropriate machinery to support these objectives must then be created and maintained. The phrase "managing officers" ordinarily connotes the top executive officers and/or the policymaking bodies, such as the board of directors in a corporation or the legislative body of a government, that are concerned with personnel management issues. Any person or group that sets pay policy or approves personnel rules is automatically included among the "managing officers" for the purposes of this book.

Basic Personnel Management Objectives

Each organization will create its own blend of personnel objectives to be sought. Despite the seeming diversity in personnel management aims and procedures, however, the collection

and critical analysis of extensive and representative data show
that there are some important personnel management objectives
that are more rather than less consistently sought and obtained.
Most employers seek to have a personnel well qualified to do the
tasks assigned them and to exercise the responsibilities given
them. The occasional employment of the poorly qualified individual by business firms or of the unproductive party adherent by
governments detracts from the universality of this primary and
basic personnel management objective but does not prevent its
wide acceptance. The same data and analysis show that the
managing officers of well-managed organizations have a strong
propensity to pay qualified personnel well but not extravagantly
and seek to make this well-qualified and well-paid personnel
highly productive and, therefore, as small as possible in number.

Personnel Management Tools

In a sizeable organization, the number of personnel management operations needed to assure even these basic objectives
is quite surprising. Personnel management confusion is inevitable
unless certain personnel management tools are well developed
and the manner of their use carefully worked out.

The first and most important of these tools is the *position
classification plan.* In it the individual positions are grouped into
homogeneous classes. The plan indicates the numbers and kinds
of positions in the organization, their nature, their similarities and
their significant differences, their organizational and geographical
location, and the relationship among them. Also very important is
a *pay plan,* based upon the position classification plan, that
provides a flat rate of pay or a graduated scale of pay for each
recognized class of positions; it is so constructed as to reflect the
pay policies, the pay levels, and the pay practices determined by
the managing officers. With these two basic personnel management tools, it becomes possible to devise and put to use other
personnel management tools needed for the effective handling of
the recruiting, in-service, and separation transactions.

While the classification of positions and the pay plan lie at
the base of the personnel system, they are not all of it. If the
managing officers want to further personnel management objec-

14

tives and to avoid confusion, their first step should be to put in writing and publicize a sound and comprehensive personnel management program. As indicated above, this program should include a clear statement of the personnel management objectives, recognizing the inevitable occurrence of the various types of personnel management transactions and the need for their orderly handling. It must recognize and list the basic personnel management tools to be developed and specify their uses. And it should contain at least broad specifications of the procedures to be used in developing and using the personnel management tools.

Second, the managing officers should state and promulgate their personnel management mandates, prescriptions, and authorizations. These directives should indicate clearly and definitely just who in the organization is to be responsible for each type of personnel management operation. The mandates should grant each responsible person the necessary authority, should specify at least broadly the procedures to be used, and should make provision for needed staff, offices, and other facilities.

Third, in the larger organizations the managing officers should establish a central personnel agency to serve as the authorized agent of the chief executive in developing personnel management tools and in using them to handle personnel management transactions.

Fourth, they should prescribe the establishment and maintenance of personnel records by the operating units and by the central personnel agency.

Fifth, the managing officers should set forth in their personnel program the relationship of the personnel agents or office with the financial, budget, housing, personnel, and other "housekeeping" agencies and officers. In a geographically scattered organization, the personnel program must be established in a way that enables it to cope with geographical problems as well.

As to the exact form of these personnel mandates, prescriptions, and authorizations, there need and can be considerable freedom of action. In the larger organizations in the public service, those considered basic must be provided by legislation. In recent years there has been a tendency to include some of the more basic personnel management mandates, prescriptions, and authorizations in the constitution or charter of the organization, and to make the legislative enactments more and more specific, covering more of the details of the personnel management program. Almost invariably, in the large government organizations, there is the mandate that the chief executive and/or the central personnel agency shall develop, adopt, and use personnel rules governing the form, content, and use of the personnel management tools; the manner of originating, considering, passing upon, and implementing the personnel management transactions; and even the detailed procedures, such as the forms to be used, the number to be prepared, and their distribution. Quite generally in large and small business organizations and in some public organizations, these matters are not provided for in the charter or through formal action of the boards of directors or legislative bodies. Too often this authority is left to the chief executive and too often also he fails to take the formal action required. Such failure accounts for much personnel management confusion.

CHAPTER 4

Observance of Personnel Management Factors

Handling the recruiting, in-service and separation personnel transactions to attain desired personnel management objectives with reasonable certainty is clearly something that should not be left to chance or to hasty improvisation. Nor is what we call common sense enough when, for instance, it is necessary to know whether an applicant for employment actually has the skill that he says he possesses. It is well to remember that good intentions and earnestness will not assure the correct answer when there is a need to determine the prevailing rate of pay for a specific job in a given location. Common sense, initiative, resourcefulness, good intentions, earnest thoughtfulness are all in order when personnel management situations call for attention and action, but something more is required when the best available answers are needed.

Over the course of the years, people have developed a number of devices to use in making decisions. One such device is to follow in the footsteps of some other person who has had to deal with a similar situation. A second device, the "common sense" course, is to determine one's own course of action on the spot. Other methods involve following one's instincts or avoiding the problem altogether by postponing a decision and action.

A superior device, and the one stressed in this book, is knowledge and consistent awareness of the foundations and working procedures of personnel management that have been developed, stated, and verified by experts in the field.

Value of Personnel Management Factors

Just what the observance or nonobservance of the working personnel management principles may mean in personnel management may be illustrated by one striking example. In many medium and large government and business organizations, the managing officers have regularly prescribed that the supervisory and administrative officers of the operating units shall, annually, semiannually, or quarterly, prepare an efficiency rating for each of their employees and report to the central personnel agency. It is to show the relative or absolute worth of the employees based upon the evaluation of their performance and conduct. Just how the supervisors are to do this is told them only briefly or not at all and, almost without exception, the employee ratings so prepared have proved to have little or no relation to performance and conduct. A single example is no proof, but doubtless the same situation occurs frequently. I recall an instance where the head of a large central personnel agency of a large public organization was visited. He called attention to two reports about the same employee that he had received a few days earlier. One was the prescribed employee rating, indicating that this particular employee was a paragon, with all the performance and conduct virtues and none of the faults. The other report was an urgent request—almost a demand—supported by convincing factual information, that immediate action be taken to separate this same employee from the service at the earliest possible moment because of his gross and patent incompetence. When the personnel head asked the supervisory officer, who had made both reports, to explain the discrepancies, he got what he considered a truthful answer: "You personnel people ask ratings of some kind periodically, so I made a copy of the last one." If too many such reports are turned in, of course, there is a weakness in the management and the organization suffers.

Hundreds and hundreds of these employee rating failures could be avoided by the observance of just two of the standard employee rating practices. One is that those who supervise a group of employees to be rated can, if properly assisted and stimulated (but seldom otherwise), report the significant facts about performance and conduct; the other is that the supervisors cannot evaluate these facts to produce reliable and valid ratings; that must be done centrally by the use of an objective scoring system. The observance of these two employee rating procedures merely prevents the type of futile employee rating system that is prevalent.

Observance of personnel management working practices, to the extent this is prescribed or permitted by the personnel management factors, reduces to a minimum the number of personnel management actions which must be based upon the less satisfactory devices of the kind described at the beginning of this chapter. Observance of these factors results in a higher degree of personnel management consistency, but the nature of personnel management operations is such that no given course of personnel management action is eternally right or wrong. The problem often is, in view of all the attendant circumstances, what course of action is the surer or the less troublesome or the least expensive in time and money in attaining the desired personnel goal. The personnel manager factors are, it should be emphasized, a *guide* for the personnel management practitioner. Wherever possible, their observance is quite sure to mean a great deal in contributing consistently and materially to the attainment of the predetermined personnel management objectives.

CHAPTER 5

Principal Personnel Management Tools

As has been pointed out in the preceding chapter, a number of personnel tools have been fashioned, tried out, proved to have much or little worth, and made available for personnel practitioners. It may seem odd to speak of concrete tools when dealing with intangible objects, but the need for diverse types of personnel tools, except possibly in very small organizations, is readily apparent to anyone familiar with the actual handling of personnel management operations. As the number of positions and employees grows, most personnel practitioners find that they lack the time and the ability to ascertain, assemble, and appraise the factual information needed—much less to memorize such things as the exact tasks performed by each of the employees, their employment histories, their organization and personnel relationships, their work performance and conduct, the conditions under which they work, their attendance, and their personal idiosyncracies. The number of positions and employees need not be great before the supervisory, administrative, and technical officers are unable to remember and match all the names and faces, much less to recall the nature and exact place in the organization of each of the positions held by the hundred. In practice it soon becomes evident that anybody who originates, considers, passes upon, and finally implements personnel transactions needs a number of aids. The well-conceived personnel tool kit contains all or most of the tools needed. They will be described briefly here; detailed discussions of the individual tools follow later in the book.

Position Classification Plan

There is no question that the basic personnel tool is the

position classification plan. Positions are established to achieve production objectives, not to make personnel operations simple and easy. Nonetheless, the position classification plan can eliminate personnel confusion by grouping the positions included in the plan into homogeneous classes. Each class contains all the positions, regardless of their department or geographical location, that are so much alike in duties, responsibilities, organization relationships, and other characteristics that they can be treated alike for pay, recruiting, induction, in-service training, employee rating, separation, and other personnel purposes. The procedure is clear and logical. A decision must be made about the classes to be recognized. Each class is given a title that should be short, descriptive, and suggestive of the duties, responsibilities, and organization relationships of the positions allocated to the class. It should also be, as far as possible, in accord with the current organization's, trade, and general occupational titling practices. The individual positions are allocated to the appropriate classes. Each class is defined with dictionary brevity and accuracy in terms of the tasks performed and by the organization relationships of those holding positions allocated to the class. Each class is also described in some detail in what are called class specifications. For personnel, budget, payroll, and other working purposes, the incumbent of each position takes the title of the class to which his position has been allocated. When this basic personnel tool has been developed, adopted and made available for use, each personnel practitioner in the organization may use it in developing whatever other personnel tools he needs to carry on his personnel work in orderly fashion. It should be stressed, however, that the development and adoption of a sound position classification plan does not in itself provide the answer to the pay, recruiting, and other personnel problems of the organization. It is the basic personnel tool, to be used in developing and using other personnel tools, and nothing more.

Pay Plan

When the position classification plan has been made available for his use, the pay technician can then proceed to develop a pay plan based upon it that implements the decisions of the managing officers about pay policies and pay levels. A good pay plan calls for a flat rate of pay or a graduated scale of pay for each of the recognized classes of positions. The rates or scales must be such as to achieve relative equity among different occupational groups and among the individual classes within any occupational group. The development, adoption, maintenance, and effective use of a sound pay plan is not an easy task, but it becomes feasible when a sound position classification plan has been developed, adopted, and made available for the use of the administrators and the pay technicians.

Recruiting Plan

The position classification plan and the pay plan having been established, the recruiting plan to be used in filling vacant positions falls into place. This may be done through transfers, promotions, demotions, or the employment of persons outside the organization. Every administrator and technician knows that successful recruiting is a complex personnel matter for which, as yet, we have no perfected tools. The formal and informal tests and batteries of tests currently being used for selective purposes have very limited value in predicting the occupational success of those selected. Tests and batteries of tests known to be reliable and valid exist for only a very few of the ten thousand classes of positions now recognized in public, business, and other organizations. The research procedures used in developing reliable and valid occupational tests are well known, but many personnel researchers have yet to acknowledge the fact and have been reluctant to undertake the needed development work. A valid test requires years of trial and error work even though some agencies and organizations offer "guaranteed validated" tests that are not dependable.

Induction and In-Service Training Plans

Regardless of the method of recruitment, the new worker in an organization, and the one transferred to a different position within an organization, needs information and assistance to become a highly productive member of the work force within a reasonable time. The handling of this area is referred to as the induction process. To give a few examples of the information he

23

needs, he must get acquainted with immediate supervisor, and find out his work assignments, his hours and place of work, and where and how to obtain supplies and equipment for his assigned tasks. When only one employee is taken on at a given time, induction matters are not difficult, of course, but when several new employees are brought in at the same time, the matter of induction presents problems that should not be ignored by supervisory officers. The necessary explanations may be supplemented by the distribution and discussion of an employee handbook. If a considerable number are inducted at the same time, a growing number of organizations have evolved formal training courses, especially when the work involved is new or unfamiliar. Here, too, no adequate in-service training plan for small or large organizations has yet been evolved that is generally usable. This factor can and is being solved and may well be left to the agencies involved, but it must not be overlooked, neglected or ignored.

When groups of employees are assembled for in-service training, it may be said that the results will be limited unless two basic conditions are met: each group must be occupationally homogeneous, in the sense that the training subject matter is common for all in the group; and the instructors must be skilled in performing the operations the training is intended to improve. Sometimes, but not always, it is possible to meet both of these requirements. It is obvious that the in-service training will not be sufficient when instructors do not have the occupational knowledge and skills needed for the occupation concerned.

Performance Rating Plan

Immediately following in-service training, the need for an employee rating plan becomes apparent. Many plans that are administratively usable produce ratings that are neither reliable nor valid. Those plans that do produce fairly reliable and valid ratings take so much of the time of the supervisory officers and the rating technicians that they can be used only for special purposes and in situations where time and temporary work stoppages are not governing. It is not being said here that each of the time-consuming and costly plans must be applied to get fair results. They are rather presented to suggest to administrators and supervisors that the questions raised here are worthy of consideration.

Preaudit and Certification of Payrolls

Another one of the personnel tools all but essential in medium-sized and large organizations is the preaudit and certification of payrolls by the central personnel agency. This particular personnel tool is widely, but not always, used in many public organizations in the United States, but the same does not exist in the business organizations. The preaudit and certification of payrolls by the central personnel agency means of course that it must audit every payroll before any officer or employee named on it can be paid for personal services, and that the personnel agency must certify to the financial officers that, with any exceptions noted, the people on the payroll have been employed in accordance with the governing laws and the prescriptions of the managing officers at the authorized rates of pay.

The preaudit and certification of payrolls by the central personnel agency serves three significant purposes. It gives assurance that the prescriptions in the personnel laws and rules about the employment of individuals at the established rates of pay are being observed. It provides the central personnel agency with up-to-date, complete, and accurate information on the personnel changes actually taking place, and it wins for the technical and clerical staffs of the central personnel agency a degree of collaboration from the operating officers in the handling of the personnel transactions.

Record-Keeping

A final basic personnel tool concerns record-keeping. Even in small organizations, some personnel records are an indispensable tool; the employer cannot rely on his memory over any extended period to recall the amount of social security taxes that has been withheld and the exact amount that must be remitted quarterly to the Internal Revenue Service or any other authorized agency. In all except very small organizations, the employment history of the employee must be readily available in written form for the employer or his agent to use in making decisions about personnel transactions. Without such records there is no certain means of knowing what to do about a proposed pay increase, a proposed granting of additional sick leave, or a proposed promotion, demotion, or transfer.

There are other personnel tools that ought to be at least mentioned: the employee safety and security plan; the leave plan (covering annual, sick, military, and other leaves); the layoff plan; the retirement plan; the removal for cause plan; the employer-employee relations plan; and the public relations plan. It is possible to handle personnel operations in more or less haphazard fashion by relying on precedents and improvisations, but each operation is more suitably handled through a carefully considered personnel tool designed and used to aid in the personnel objectives of the organization.

Effective Use of Personnel Tools

1. In sum, there are four pieces of cautionary advice concerning the use of personnel management tools. The personnel tool ought to be used principally for the purpose for which it is intended and not for something else. If the recruiting tool, for example, is used to hire members of particular groups or parties rather than those who are the best qualified occupationally of all those available, then its usefulness as a tool is lost.

2. It may not be expected that any personnel tool, however competent its user may be, is perfect. No personnel tool is completely accurate for it deals with people who have all kinds of temperaments, characteristics and abilities.

3. The existing personnel tools do make it possible for those who use them to more easily, speedily, and certainly accomplish the things they are trying to do. Without question most of the present-day personnel tools reduce many personnel problems to manageable proportions.

4. Good personnel tools ultimately call for a good workman. The administrator, the rating technician, the immediate supervisor may fret about the failure of the others who have a part in the action taken and the end result, but they are all involved. The employee rating tool is but one part of the employment process and its role is essential for achieving the desired results.

CHAPTER 6

The Individual Position

The position, a particular group or series of tasks, exists independent of a person. The employee does at times recognize the existence of the intangible position, and its aggregate of tasks to be performed by the person holding it, when he uses such expressions as "I got a new job today." The employer, too, recognizes that the position exists; in a well-ordered budget, for example, positions and not persons are listed, both in the document itself and in the supporting data. In some government agencies and business organizations the terms "establishment" or "the established list" or the "position list" are coming into use.

The managing officers of an organization who have the responsibility for authorizing and establishing positions as a part of their general administrative work should take three steps. First, they should consciously and deliberately, by specific action, authorize the establishment of each and every position they consider to be needed in the organization. Second, they should require that the tasks and the working relationships allocated to any position be recorded. Third, they should give any authorized position a short, descriptive name or title.

It must be remembered, however, that as the work program, the internal organization, and the operating procedures of the organization change, the positions must and do change. Furthermore, the nature of a position is influenced, for good or for bad, by the capabilities of the incumbents. This evolution of positions must occur. The "establishment" or "established list" or "position list" does not prevent it or do a great deal to retard it. And, except in an organization that is very static indeed, it is desirable that this continuous flux go on. The answer is not to prevent changes, but to ascertain what they are and to record them.

CHAPTER 7

Individual and Group Roles in Personnel Management

Once the concept of personnel management operations has been worked out, defined, and explained, it is possible to guide those who carry on personnel management activities in their respective organizations. These may be full-time personnel specialists or others who spend only part of their time on personnel matters. They include the managing officers, the individual employees, the department supervisory and administrative officers, the chief executive, the personnel technicians and their assistants, and the higher officers or technicians in the other "housekeeping" agencies.

Role of the Managing Officers

For high-ranking or managing officers, personnel management activities are merely one part of their varied tasks and responsibilities. (The term "managing officers" lacks the sanction of wide use; it has been used because a name is needed for this concept inherent in any analysis of personnel management.) They participate from time to time in these additional personnel matters:

1. Deciding upon all significant personnel objectives and policies of the organization.

2. Determining and expressing or at least passing upon the basic personnel mandates, prescriptions and organizations, and seeing that they are implemented.

3. Providing for the establishment of the central personnel agency and defining its powers, duties, and responsibilities.

4. Seeing that the personnel management activities of the organization are effectively coordinated with the operating activities of the various departments; making final decisions when the operating officers and the personnel management officers are unable to agree about personnel management activities and the manner of handling them.

5. Coordinating the activities of the several "housekeeping" units when necessary to assure proper collaboration and to prevent conflicts and inaction.

6. Providing needed funds, staff, quarters, equipment, supplies, and other facilities for the central personnel agency and for any officer outside the central personnel agency whose work assignment is primarily personnel management.

7. Taking any additional actions that may be needed to achieve the personnel objectives.

From this outline of the powers, duties, and responsibilities of the managing officers, it may be inferred that this category includes those who draft and adopt the constitution or the charter of the organization, the members of the legislative body in the public service and of the board of directors in business organizations, the chief executive in organizations of all types, and the group or single officer having the power to make binding personnel rules (often, in the public service, the civil service commission or the head of the personnel unit). The top personnel officer is increasingly being made more responsible for some of these administrative duties listed. But, in any organization, the chief executive, probably more than any other individual or any one group, normally determines how personnel management operations are handled and what the personnel management end products turn out to be. He may all but nullify personnel management mandates and prescriptions simply by neglect or by doing nothing deliberately. Or, by understanding and vigorous action, he may take the measures needed to fulfill personnel management expectations.

Role of Department Supervisors

The department supervisory and administrative officers, as well as the executives, have numerous and important personnel management responsibilities. If there is no personnel management program for the organization as a whole, then the responsibility falls on the head of each department, who, with the aid of his assistants, must devise and administer a plan and policy of his own. If the managing officers have determined personnel objectives and policies for the whole organization, have prescribed a personnel management program, and have given the departments a definite personnel management assignment to be implemented in accordance with prescribed procedures, then each department head and his supervisory and administrative assistants have numerous but fairly definite personnel management tasks to attend to. Even when the managing officers have established a central personnel agency to aid in implementation of the prescribed program, each department head and his assistants still have much personnel management work to do.

Roles of Specific Agents Within an Organization

The roles of the principal "housekeeping" agencies of any organization that, in addition to the central personnel agency, include those concerned with the preparation of the budget estimates and the execution of the adopted budget are: keeping financial records and making payments; purchasing, storing, and distributing supplies and equipment; and providing and maintaining working quarters. In the discharge of these joint duties it is of course important that the budget agency and the central personnel agency both keep accurate records of the positions authorized and established, that they use the same titles for the individual positions, that each keep the other informed about position changes, that each recognize the proper role of the other in the establishment of positions and pay plans, that each take pains to

31

prevent the needless duplication of personnel records, and that they avoid requiring duplicate personnel reports from the operating officers.

The personnel technicians and their clerical assistants handle the technical tasks involved in developing the personnel tools and using them to assure application of applicable personnel factors, as well as the prescribed procedures in the personnel laws and rules when personnel transactions are originated, considered, decided, and carried out. These technicians may be part of the technical staff of the central personnel agency, of a personnel consulting firm, or of some other outside group.

It may be said that the managing or supervisory officers are likely to be amateurs in personnel management. The technical people, on the other hand, are and must be experienced and trained in their work; they must be grounded in the science and skilled in the art of personnel management. Except for the technological researchers, the technician should spend his working time doing personnel management tasks in accordance with applicable governing personnel management principles and with the procedures outlined in personnel laws and rules. He needs to be aware of the significant environment factors and of the opposing forces that affect his work. Normally he has frequent contacts with others who are not personnel technicians but who participate in one way or another in personnel management operations. This means that he must be something of a diplomat, able to establish and maintain working relationships with those participants who find it uncomfortable to follow the essential personnel management principles and prescribed procedures.

Role of the Employee

The employee himself has an essential role in practically every transaction affecting his position, actual or potential. His participation begins with recruiting, continues through in-service operations, and ends only when he is finally separated from the position and possibly from the organization.

The essential role of the employee in the personnel transactions that concern him and his position is apparent. There can be no establishment of the employer-employee relationship without his collaboration except under unusual circumstances, such as the wartime draft for military service. To some extent, his rate of pay, his place and hours of work, his working conditions, and other matters must be explained to his satisfaction before he becomes an employee; after his employment, his consent must often be obtained before changes are made in these conditions. Usually he is given some freedom in choosing his vacation dates. He has a part in determining the time and conditions of his retirement, and he is free to resign when he wishes. He has some part in disciplinary actions affecting him or in his proposed dismissal. Even in employee ratings, he must be informed of his superior's appraisal if he and his employer are to make effective use of them.

Good personnel management becomes difficult, uncertain, or even impossible to the extent that any group or individual usurps or ignores the proper role of the other. Each has an important and necessary part in the effective handling of nearly every type of personnel transaction and each has to play the part to achieve good personnel management.

CHAPTER 8

Physical and Social Influences on Personnel Management Operations

Because in every field of human endeavor there are opposing factors and forces that place limitations upon what human beings can accomplish, it seems worthwhile to enumerate and explain a number of the more significant situations that powerfully influence personnel management operations. In contrast with some other fields, most of these influences are social—only geography is a physical item in personnel management.

Ignorance of Personnel Management Factors

First is the difficulty of getting managing officers, their assistants, employees, and even many personnel technicians to become aware of and take due account of the facts of personnel life. Most are only dimly aware that there is a science of personnel management and an art based upon and derived from it. Of those who are aware, a majority are skeptical about the worth of any such science and art to them as they dispose of the personnel transactions that they cannot escape.

Second is the widespread unwillingness of the individual personnel practitioner dealing with a specific personnel management transaction to consistently use the appropriate personnel management factor or procedure that he knows and whose validity he accepts.

Physical Separation

The third item is the geographical dispersion of the physical plant and work force that often occurs in medium-sized and large government and business organizations. With increases in numbers of employees and buildings, or with employment of field workers and salesmen, the personnel problems become more and more complex. When there are physical plants and working forces in geographically scattered areas, the whole personnel management system has to be retailored to avoid confusion and inconsistencies. Experience has shown that an organization, however large and however scattered geographically, should have one unified personnel management system with a headquarters staff to provide personnel policies, procedures, and tools. An administrative staff is also needed in each area or district to participate in handling personnel transactions occurring in that area or district and to maintain close working relations between each area and headquarters staff.

Public Apathy and Social Problems

The widespread apathy of voters and taxpayers about personnel matters in government organizations, and of stockholders in businesses, is another influence in personnel management operations. A vocal minority of voters have been remarkably successful in getting government personnel laws, but their interest has not extended to assuring that the laws are subsequently enforced. Stockholders follow the same pattern. This type of apathy on the part of the public, characteristic of both business and public organizations, discourages and delays the extension of any superior type of personnel management operations.

On the other hand, public interest can adversely and powerfully influence personnel management when it results in the mixing of personnel and social problems. Injecting a social problem into personnel management operations seldom or never solves it. A good example of this concerns the U.S. government's preferential hiring of veterans. We owe our veterans a great deal, but this is neither the way to solve the employment and rehabilitation problems of the veteran, nor the way to operate an effective personnel system.

Foreman Autonomy

The granting of personnel autonomy to foremen and other

36

supervisory officers creates a sixth situation that is bound to have some impact on personnel management operations. Foreman autonomy limits the opportunity for the capable personnel technician to use his talents and skills effectively. The absence of such opportunity has discouraged many talented people who want to work with people and has produced a scarcity of competent personnel technicians; therefore, when managing officers of government or business organizations do decide to attack their personnel management problems in earnest, they have considerable difficulty in finding capable personnel management technicians. The personnel manpower situation is further complicated in response to this need by the fact that too many people, inadequately trained in sound and recognized personnel management working procedures, have entered the field. They do not know the science or the art involved and will not undertake the painstaking technical work involved in fashioning personnel tools and using them to apply personnel management procedures consistently. They distract attention from basic technical personnel problems by their ineptitude in coming to grips with the fundamental aspects of these problems.

Pressure Groups and Social Fluctuations

An eighth possible influence concerns the activities of individuals and pressure groups who interest themselves in personnel management operations. Included are groups representing taxpayers, stockholders, veterans, business and civil interests of various types, numerous trades and professions, voters, and ethnic and racial classes. These groups may be well-meaning and seek to perform valuable functions, and some of them do, but more often than not they emphasize only parts of what is most likely a larger issue. As stated above, mixing personnel and social problems, no matter what type, rarely helps the situation.

The spirit and manner of the times constitute a ninth powerful influence on personnel management operations. When war comes, for example, there is a strong tendency in both government and business organizations to ignore the sound and proved personnel management guides at the very time when their intelligent and consistent observance is most needed. In boom times few employees or employers want to be hemmed in by troublesome personnel rules and techniques; when economic depression strikes, then personnel palliatives are sought.

Employee Skepticism

A tenth situation involves the fact that employees themselves are often skeptical or doubtful about the effects of personnel management. The realization that many employees dislike and distrust their activities causes personnel technicians to wonder whether it is all worthwhile. That state of mind, when and if it comes, may of itself constitute a major force making good personnel management difficult if not impossible to achieve.

Poor Advice and Vague Objectives

Seeking personnel advice and assistance from the wrong source is an eleventh possible source of trouble. It is a curious phenomenon that our largest governments and many of our big business organizations, though themselves little given to making use of the findings of personnel management, are too willing to give personnel management advice and assistance to those who come to them for guidance. The consequences of this collaboration are rarely constructive.

Finally, the failure to state and define the personnel management objective of the organization is very common. In most organizations, the managing officers have in mind, at least vaguely, a personnel goal that is briefly expressed as a personnel well qualified, well, but not extravagantly paid, and so utilized as to be highly productive and therefore requiring as few as possible in number. But in many large and small organizations, and in many subdivisions of those well-managed as a whole, such a personnel management objective is completely ignored or cast aside for long or short periods when it is found to be inconvenient. Personnel management operations are often carried on through improvisations, precedents, personal desires and feelings, and expedience, with limited regard for the achieving of carefully thought out objectives. While it is axiomatic that the attainment of defined personnel management objectives should be governing, such, in practice, has not been the case.

PART II

THE GROWTH AND STATUS
OF PERSONNEL MANAGEMENT
AS A SCIENCE AND ART

Introduction to Part II

In any effort to present the principles of personnel management, it seems necessary, in discussing the growth and current status of the *science* and *art* of personnel management, to define and illustrate the exact sense in which the words are used. Both have a number of meanings that are widely accepted.

The generally accepted definition of science concerns a body of classified knowledge or facts that may be used to describe the actions and reactions of items when they are used in certain situations or ways.

A field of knowledge need not be concerned primarily with physical things to be regarded as something less than a science. Nor is a particular field of knowledge regarded as something less than a science because it is concerned with social phenomena, or because the results when put to use are lacking in precision in some measure. Instead, certain requirements, though not wholly objective, constitute what we may now consider the criteria to be termed a science:

1. There must be a large body of systematically arranged knowledge concerning some subject or group of related subjects.

2. This body of information must be factual, verified, extensive, and representative.

3. There must be a statement of reliable, valid, significant, and usable conclusions based upon and derived from the results of careful, methodical, and critical analyses.

In addition to the science of personnel management, there is an art based upon it. Once a science is developed, with its body of factual information and its conclusions clearly stated, the way to improvements in practice becomes understandable. Others may reject our persistence here, but there is a need for a term indicating the body of methods, tools, practices, and devices used in carrying on day-to-day operations in such a manner as to give reasonable assurance of success in achieving objectives. In the absence of any better term, the word art is used for this purpose and is defined as: the methods and practices based upon a science that, when consistently used, give reasonable assurance of achieving desired objectives in a selected field.

40

CHAPTER 9

The Growth of Personnel Management in the United States

Personnel management is not a new term; nor is it a newly discovered relationship. It is as old as human relationships and began when there were first employer-employee relationships. It is inevitable that from time to time some personnel pioneer would put in writing the current personnel practices of his social unit; in documents as ancient as the Mosaic law and the codes of Hammurabi one may find references to treatment of servants and soldiers. While the recorded practices do not constitute a science or an art, they do represent some of the first steps in such a development.

Civil Service Reform Movement

In America, a pertinent step in the development of the field was the Civil Service Reform movement. In 1883, following the assassination of President Garfield in 1881 by a disappointed officer seeker, the national government and the states of New York and Massachusetts enacted personnel laws applying to a considerable number of their civil servants. In the next thirty years similar personnel laws were enacted in a few other states and in some local governments also. These early laws had as their primary objective the circumventing of the political spoils system of office filling. To achieve this it was necessary to name or classify positions to the extent that "examinations" could be devised and held to weed out applicants who were not qualified for positions in the public service. A central personnel agency was set up to handle day-to-day transactions and provide enforcement. However ineptly these personnel laws were administered they did reduce the all but complete turnover of the employed personnel in these governments when administrations changed. Oddly enough, business organizations, with few exceptions, took little notice of or interest in the personnel movement going on in government and continued their old practice of foremen hiring the rank and file employees.

The real movement toward the use of the civil service or merit system began to take shape in the early years of the present century and that interest and extension marked the beginning of thirty years of real progress. While England, as well as some other European countries, had been making substantial progress in the use of the merit principle, the creation of what may be called the first real public personnel law was developed, adapted and put into effect in New Zealand. This new law seemed to have little if any effect on the movement in the United States. So far as can be determined few people interested in the improvement of public administration by and through a more sensible handling of public personnel knew anything about the New Zealand action.

Here at home more and more citizens were interesting themselves in our governmental problems and there was a sense of change or reform in the air. In the first ten years of the present century a few of our states and more of our larger cities adopted and put into effect civil service or merit system laws. The personnel agencies were making some progress in finding their place in the administrative picture, but they had not found the way to cope with what we now call the classification problem. Appointing authorities were besieged by and for prospective appointees who had special or unusual experience and background or connections.

The Influence of E. O. Griffenhagen

In Chicago the problem of special interest groups had reached such proportions that the city Civil Service Commission was called upon in 1909 to find a man to deal with the problem of applicants pressuring the chairman of the Chicago City Council

Finance Committee. The man selected was E. O. Griffenhagen, who eventually set a milestone in personnel management history.

The plan that Griffenhagen developed grouped the thousands of positions in the city service into something more than a thousand occupational classes. Each class included all the positions in the whole city service that were so much alike as to work assignments, responsibilities, organization relationships, geographical location, and other characteristics that they could properly be treated alike for pay, recruiting and other purposes. Each class of positions was given a title that was at once short, descriptive, and as far as possible in accordance with accepted trade practices; this title was used in the budget and in the personnel documents and records. For each of the recognized classes of positions, a flat rate or a graduated scale of pay such as to bring about relative equity in and among the varied occupational groups was developed, adopted, and put to use in budget and personnel operations. Upward and downward pay adjustments within the graduated scale of pay for any class were made on the basis of carefully stated standards. These arrangements were so significant and effective that they were widely accepted and remain today as the cornerstone of personnel management.

The established classes of positions were used not only for pay purposes, but also in handling recruiting, in-service, and separation transactions. Personnel rules were written and adopted stating the procedures for developing and using the personnel tools in day-to-day personnel transactions. They were not only adopted, they were effectively administered. Needed personnel records were established, maintained, and used in carrying on the technical operations, especially the preaudit and certification of payrolls. The technical and clerical staffs needed by the Civil Service Commission were built up and trained to do their assigned tasks effectively. What and how it was done is described in the *Annual Report of the Chicago Civil Service Commission for 1913;* this document is long out of print but may be found in libraries that have a collection of personnel literature.

The initial Chicago personnel work brought the handling of personnel operations in this country to the level of what we now call a science and an art. The new personnel guides and operating procedures were put to use in the three park districts of Chicago.

Leaving the Chicago city service, Mr. Griffenhagen organized and directed a personnel consulting organization that, in the next twenty years, introduced this new type of personnel operations in numerous state and local government services, in the national government services of Canada and the United States, and, in considerably modified and limited forms, to some business firms. As the years passed, other personnel consulting organizations helped to extend the movement in all parts of the country.

Charles P. Messick
and the Bureau of Public Personnel Administration

It was Charles P. Messick, the executive officer of the New Jersey Civil Service Commission, who took the lead in bringing about the wide acceptance and use of the "Griffenhagen" type of personnel management. He took the steps needed to fill in the gaps, eliminate the flaws, and add refinements. Messick made the leading personnel practitioners in the public service aware of the need for extensive investigative, research, and training work in the personnel field.

Messick began working for the State of New Jersey in 1910, advancing to Assistant Chief Examiner and, in 1917, to Chief Executive Officer of the Department. He succeeded in implementing a proper position classification system, together with a pay plan for the state service, and began using them in handling the recruiting, in-service, and separation transactions. He built up the needed technical and clerical staffs, and assigned them to productive tasks. He brought about a complete revision of the personnel laws and the adoption of realistic and constructive personnel rules. He designed, installed, maintained, and properly used needed personnel records. Messick established working relations with the legislative bodies and their committees interested in personnel operations, particularly the appropriations committee; the chief executive; the other "housekeeping" agencies; the department heads and their assistants; the employee organizations and groups; the political organizations; and civic and business groups interested in personnel operations. These and other personnel activities made New Jersey outstanding in the handling of its personnel work.

As an active member and from time to time as president of the Civil Service Assembly of the United States and Canada (now the International Personnel Management Association), Messick led the body, in 1920, to approve the concept that the development, adoption, and proper use of a position classification plan is the basic tool in carrying on large-scale personnel operations effectively. He had a leading part in obtaining funds to finance the carrying on of personnel research, publishing, and servicing work through a new organization called the Bureau of Public Personnel Administration, which was established in 1922. He became the most active and influential member of the "advisory board" of the agency, which directed its activities, and for most of the Bureau's active life was its chairman.

The Bureau served a number of purposes. Its staff visited members of the Civil Service Assembly and others, supplied them with personnel information they requested, and gave technical assistance and advice about improved methods of handling technical personnel operations. The Bureau was active in developing and ascertaining the validity of tests and batteries of tests to be used in predicting the occupational success of those considered for employment. It developed a system for public employee ratings, based upon the work of J. B. Probst of St. Paul, and collected significant personnel information from many sources, disseminating it through the Bureau's monthly publication, *Public Personnel Studies*. The Bureau became the agency that drew together the personnel management people all over America, encouraging them to work together and pointing the way. The great progress in the field of personnel management in the 1920's was largely the result of this agency.

Government Leads in Innovations

Although it has long been accepted as fact that business organizations moved ahead of the government in handling its personnel problems, the evidence is everywhere that this was not the case. Business followed, it did not lead, in the use of personnel management practices in the formative, developing period of growth. Currently business has accepted the improved and enlightened personnel management practices and is using the basic

45

foundation on which personnel operations must be based. It has adopted and adapted to its own use many gadgets and refinements of the personnel management policies, such as standardized tests for manual dexterity, proneness to accidents and mechanical aptitude, safety measures, the coffee break, the suggestion box, the exit interview, the family welfare adviser, and the like. These are all valuable personnel devices and belong in any sound and comprehensive personnel system, but they are refinements, not the essence of the matter.

In 1918 the classification of the civil service was undertaken by Congressional direction under a Joint Congressional Commission, and in 1920 that Commission proposed a number of constructive measures. A few batteries of tests of proved reliability and validity for use in selecting many of the applicants to be employed in the postal service were constructed, and the personnel rules dating back to the last century were revised in some important respects. The Classification Act, enacted by Congress in 1923, dealt with the classification of civilian positions in the headquarters area, established the machinery for determining pay rates, and vested administrative authority in a newly created body called the Personnel Classification Board. Later on, the jurisdiction of the Board was extended to the civilian "field" positions.

Unfortunately, the records show widespread disregard for the provisions of the Act. Pay changes were apparently made with little regard for equity or policy, and confusion rather than order became the pattern. This situation brought about the abolition of the Board in 1932 and the transfer of its functions and powers to the Civil Service Commission. But the same difficulties remained and in 1938 President Roosevelt, by executive order, established bureau personnel units within the departments and gave these bureau units broad powers, particularly in classification matters. While this was a step that many personnel students and technicians at the time regarded as highly desirable, in practice it has not proved of value or practical use.

Decline of the Growth of Personnel Management

During the 1930's it had thus become apparent that, while the science and the art of personnel management had won acceptance in certain quarters, there were large deficiencies and gaps in the techniques and too few governments, businesses and educational institutions paid the successful practices heed. Here and there powerful employee organizations joined in the drafting and enactment of advanced personnel legislation, and assisted in bringing about its effective administration. In this period, too, the industrial unions were active in working out sound classifications for a number of the craft types of workers and in forcing both government and business employers to recognize and use such classifications in carrying on their personnel work.

The personnel optimists were greatly encouraged, nonetheless. They were inclined to overlook the deficiencies and the gaps in the science and the art, or not to recognize that they were at the beginning of a process, rather than having reached the goal. They seemed not to recognize that too many governments, businesses and educational institutions had yet to realize the significance of the foundations or working procedures that had been developed. Our optimists were inclined to regard themselves as permanent settlers in the new land of personnel management when in fact they were yet still pioneers.

Symbolically, the progress that had been made in personnel management was halted by the Great Depression. The Bureau of Public Personnel Administration lost its financial support and the staff was forced to find work where it could. Messick accepted the presidency of the Assembly again; he had the records shipped to him and carried on, using his own funds in keeping the Assembly, the Bureau and his own demonstration in New Jersey alive.

The field of personnel management has never really recovered from the combined effects of the depression, World War II, and the following period of rapid economic growth, inflation, increasing automation and, in general, rapid social changes. The Civil Service Assembly has been reestablished, but the new organization, now called the International Personnel Management Association, has taken a different course, of necessity. Previously, the Bureau was funded and could engage in progressive research; now it must earn its own way and must therefore direct its activities toward that end.

Turning to the business world, the same questions and uncertainties remain. Some large business organizations have recognized the importance and the necessity of adapting and putting into practice the principles of personnel management. A goodly number have set up what we in government would call elaborate and expensive programs, but it must be said that a limited number only have developed and used the basic personnel tools and rules for their use, for classification procedures, and what we believe to be a sound pay plan. Yet personnel management workers in the whole private enterprise field know and have access to all of the knowledge and procedures that have proved useful, time-saving and economical.

The science and the art of personnel management do remain in existence, however, and numerous personnel officers realize this and are using them effectively. There are signs, too, that a personnel resurgence may be in the offing. When and if it comes, the science and the art of personnel management, and their uses, are in the records and remain as useful as when they were first formulated and practiced. Indeed, the editing and publishing of this book now is primarily to insure that these records are available for all.

CHAPTER 10

The Current Status of Personnel Management

The development of any science, and the art based upon it, is almost invariably uneven. This chapter will attempt to deal concisely with the strong and weak points of the personnel management movement as it is now practiced.

Successful Personnel Management Developments

One successful aspect has been the development and statement of the personnel program and assignment; of the personnel mandates, prescriptions, and authorizations; and of the preparation, adoption, and use of the personnel rules and regulations. There are differences in method, but many specific plans exist, and the person given the responsibility for this area has a choice between plans, or parts of plans, that have already proved their worth in practice.

Other successful developments have concerned the adoption and use of the classification and the pay plans, for all or nearly all positions in the organization. These are the basic personnel tools. The process begins with ascertaining, recording, and checking the tasks performed by those holding the individual positions that are classified. The next steps concern determining the classes of positions to be recognized, the title to be given each recognized class, and the definitions and descriptions of the several classes. Individual positions are then all allocated to their appropriate classes.

Management must next develop pay policies for the central personnel agency to administer, taking into consideration pay practices in the organization and in other government and business organizations in the geographical area. Another policy to be set is the extent to which flat rates of pay or graduated scales of pay are to be used for the classes in the different occupational groups. Neither the classification nor the pay plans are static creations, however; changes must be noted and eventually taken into consideration. There are procedures of proven worth for making the initial adjustments in the rate of pay of individual officers and employees, and informing them of what has been done. The administration of the adopted pay plan, after the initial pay adjustments have been made, is not easy, but the manner of its implementation is well known. The same is true in establishing rates or scales of pay for newly established classes. A particularly perplexing administrative pay problem is that of making upward and downward adjustments in the pay of individuals within the limits of adopted scales of pay. The one thing missing here is reliable and valid employee ratings. Without them—and they seldom exist—there are not satisfactory courses available.

These three techniques—the form and content of the personnel assignment and program; the development, adoption, and use of the position classification plan; and the development, adoption, and use of the pay plan—represent the principal steps in the development of the science and the art of personnel management, but there are several others. Another procedure found to be useful is the development, in public and private organizations having central personnel agencies, of procedures that bring together the participation of the representatives of the central personnel agency and the chief executive in the handling of the day-to-day personnel transactions. The pioneers in the field clearly realized that the agency must have a part in adjustments, promotions, demotions, transfers, layoffs, removals for cause, and other transactions, and lead the way in matters of the governing personnel laws, rules and regulations of the other units concerned.

A corollary of this is the practice of the central personnel agency establishing and maintaining working relations with various individuals and groups, and developing and using procedures and methods for so doing. In addition to those already mentioned (employees, their immediate supervisors, and other operating officers) the individuals and groups include the department heads and their principal assistants; the chief executive; the legislative body or the board of directors; legislative committees and their members; committees established by the board of directors; the representatives of the employee groups; the representatives of the interested trade, professional, civic, and business groups; influential members of the political parties in the public service and of taxpayer groups; and, in business organizations, influential stockholders. The personnel relationships between the central agency and these other groups are significant not only in personnel matters but also in financial, organization, production, distribution, and other activities.

Another practice found to be successful, primarily in the public service, is the preaudit and certification of payrolls by the central personnel agency before payments for personnel services may be made. This requirement serves two principal personnel purposes: it provides the central personnel agency with accurate, complete, and up-to-date information about what goes on in the personnel field, and it assures all concerned with the operation and functioning of the government that in the personnel field, at least, the payrolls are controlled and this can be verified.

A final marked success, although there are others that could be mentioned, is the use of reliable and valid trait tests, borrowed for the most part from the psychologists, educators, and others. These tests are used for screening purposes in recruiting work and for predicting occupational success. Among the traits that may be measured with a high degree of reliability and validity are abstract intelligence, mechanical aptitude, mechanical ability, manual dexterity, work interests, ability to use correct English, ability to understand, remember, and carry out oral and written directions, and proneness to accidents. No tests, or series of tests, are perfect, but substantial progress has been made, if not in predicting occupational success, then in screening out many potential failures.

51

CHAPTER 11

Deficiencies and Gaps in the Field of Personnel Management

Recognition of the successes in the development of the science and the art of personnel management, however impressive they have been, should not obscure the almost equally impressive deficiencies and gaps.

The most obvious problem has been the failure to develop batteries of tests that are both reliable and valid for use in predicting the occupational success of those who are considered for employment. All told, there are in our government and business organizations some ten thousand occupational groups, or classes of positions, that are recognized. Each is so unlike the others that separate and distinct batteries of tests are needed for consistently successful recruiting results, but reliable and valid tests have been developed for only a few of these classes of positions. In the absence of tests known to have predictive value, tests and batteries of tests of unknown worth are all but universally used when recruiting work is to be carried on. Enough research has been done to show quite conclusively that a sizable fraction of these have limited predictive value, many are little more than rituals, and a sizable proportion have no predictive value—a harsh statement to be sure, but difficult to prove false.

Yet with the absence of reliable and valid appraisals, expressed in the form of employee ratings, of the performance of those employed, there is no ready means of knowing how effective or ineffective many of these selective tests are. We now know quite well how to go about the development of a battery of tests having reliability and real and not merely face validity for any given class of positions. The development work is slow and tedious because it is difficult to obtain the valid appraisals of performance that constitute the only known criterion, but such development work should be done.

The second deficiency easily can be inferred from the recruiting results—the absence of any administratively usable system of employee ratings that produces reliable and valid appraisals of the performance of individual employees. As has already been mentioned, J. B. Probst, in the St. Paul merit system department, first working alone and later in collaboration with the Bureau of Public Personnel Administration, discovered, stated, and applied most of the basic principles and developed many usable procedures. Among other things, he worked out a rather elaborate performance report to be used in ascertaining and recording significant facts about each employee's performance during a specific work period, and an objective system for evaluating the report to produce a rating in numerical form. Probst made the fatal error of keeping his system for numerical rating a close secret, however. In practice, moreover, supervisors became unwilling to give unfavorable reports when it became clear that they led to disagreeable employee personnel actions. We now know fairly well how to bring about the needed advances and refinements in performance and it seems probable that the development of reliable and valid batteries of tests for predicting occupational success will lag until reliable and valid appraisals of performance that will be accepted become available.

Personnel managers have also failed to develop administratively usable personnel performance rating systems for the small and intermediate-sized organizations. The informal methods of handling personnel management operations begin to break down when the number of positions in the organization reaches even a hundred, for the simple reason that few supervisory or administrative officers will record the facts needed for personnel decision-making. Without a minimum personnel staff, with proper authority and facilities, there is no known means of developing the basic personnel tools and then using them in the effective handling of day-to-day personnel transactions. Thus far, few government or business organizations, when the number of employees continues around the hundred positions figure, have been able or seen fit to assign a worker and give him the necessary authority, and provide him with the necessary facilities to carry on this work. This neglect becomes more costly as the number of positions in the organization grows to five hundred, a thousand, or more.

A similar lack of effective procedures exists with the problem of making upward and downward pay adjustments within the adopted scale of pay. The mere existence of a graduated scale of pay for a given class, rather than a flat rate, necessarily implies that there are to be pay adjustments from time to time within that scale. There is also an implication that such adjustments, upward and downward, will be based upon all the factors considered significant. Those who devised and first used the graduated scale of pay assumed that at least two factors would consistently be taken into account in making pay adjustments: work performance and length of time served at the existing rate. In practice, this premise, or anything remotely resembling it, has been almost universally abandoned. This is partly because the lack of reliable and valid employee ratings has left those who handle pay adjustments without the basic personnel tool they need. As a result upward pay adjustments at stated periods have become all but automatic after some designated period of service at the existing rate. And the downward pay adjustment within the adopted scale of pay has practically disappeared. In the absence of reliable and valid employee ratings, no solution for this pay failure is in sight.

The general retention in the public service of the personnel commission with administrative powers as the actual or nominal head of the central personnel agency constitutes the fifth major deficiency in the development of personnel management. Business organizations, it should be noted, have uniformly avoided this mistake. The creation of the United States Civil Service Commission in 1883 was the earliest experiment of this type; since then this example has been widely followed in personnel work and in other government fields. From the beginning in 1883 to the present day, the personnel commission, wherever it exists in the public service, has been a burden rather than a help. It contributes little or nothing to the development and implementing of sound and comprehensive personnel systems, distracts attention from the personnel problems to be dealt with, and interposes delays in the making of necessary decisions. Even though Messick made his records in the administrative field with a commission, he confesses that he did so by developing his own power, always greater than that of his commission. He now urges the abandonment of the commission, for a director with cabinet status and pay as the head of the personnel department.

The present lack of productive personnel research work is a sixth failure and one that affects all other aspects of the field. From the very beginning, productive personnel research work has been carried on almost exclusively by individual personnel practitioners impatient with the unsatisfactory results attained so far in some phase of their technical work. Often these practitioners have borrowed end products, procedures, and devices from the psychologists, statisticians, educators, and others. For some years now productive personnel research has been conspicuous mostly by its absence. It is hoped that this situation will change. Certainly there is pressing need for such research in order to produce an administratively usable system of reliable and valid employee ratings and to develop batteries of tests to predict successful occupational performance.

The seventh marked deficiency is the shortage of capable personnel administrators and technicians at all levels, and particularly in the lowest professional level. While the universities are now offering courses in personnel management, the need for such trained administrators and technicians has grown so fast and has become so important in the administrative plans of both public and private enterprise that we have barely touched the surface of that need. The alternative has been the slow and expensive alternative of training the workers on the job.

The eighth deficiency is our inability to keep the adopted classification plan up to date without extensive and expensive overhauling at intervals of two to five years. So frequent and significant are departmental changes in internal organization, in operating procedures and methods, in staffing, in physical plant and equipment, in the work assignments of individual officers and employees, and in other respects that the classification plan that is accurate at the time of its development and adoption becomes seriously misleading within a period as short as six months unless it is surveyed regularly. The need for some classification changes is reported to the central personnel agency technician in charge of classification matters by the operating officers. The need for some other classification changes may be discovered in the preaudit of payrolls, and everybody in the organization hears about such changes as the opening or closing of a shop or a branch unit. Capable personnel technicians discover many position changes as they confer with the operating officers and the representatives of employee groups and as they personally observe working conditions. Numerous position changes do not come to the attention of the classifiers as soon as they occur, however, and slowly but inevitably the classification inaccuracies accumulate until the classification plan is out of joint. This is only to say that any classification plan is a living, changing thing. Its currency marks the level of its use and value.

Another deficiency of considerable import is our failure, up to this time, to evaluate the relative worth of many of the varying procedures and tools when more than one is known to have value in achieving desired personnel ends. On the application form, for example, the person seeking employment is usually asked to record his work history. But the directions given him, the space set aside for his answers, and the form in which the answers are to be recorded vary widely. We are asked what type of directions and spacing most consistently elicits the information desired and used? Our answer is that we do not yet know. There are literally hundreds of different procedures for handling different personnel management operations, and refinements must be made before personnel management proceeds to a new stage of development.

In general, there is widespread disregard of the science and the art of personnel management, in whole or in part, in organizations of all sizes and types. And there is not now available any reasonably complete and technically accurate exposition of the science and the art of personnel management for the use of personnel practitioners, teachers, students, and others interested in this field. Yet, this book is based upon the conviction that we have made progress in the development of a science and an art of personnel management and that the discoveries are usable and useful in carrying on personnel management operations.

CHAPTER 12

The Formal Teaching
of Personnel Management

Like many other arts and sciences, the skills and refinements attached to this discipline literally grew up. For many years after the art, if not the science, of personnel management was known there was no formal recognition of it and no effort to provide training for those engaged in, or contemplating entering into, that work. It was a process of learning by doing. During the immediate past generation some of the most effective workers and technicians gave little thought to the problem of professional training. In fact, they gave little if any thought to the factors behind the procedures they themselves had worked out and were then following.

The questions of what constitutes a comprehensive curricula for personnel management training has always been an issue. We would say that it is not entirely settled yet. There is no argument as to the difficulty of the task, nor of its importance. In the decades of the teens and twenties the few personnel consulting organizations took the leading part in the training of personnel administrators and technicians in classification and pay work, to ensure that the results of their work would be credited as both useful and valuable. This was a good way of advertising their services. Workers in the personnel group began to discuss the work of the consultants and the application of the ideas involved. The personnel workers with imagination made their way to the top and the use of the tools and the procedures proposed began to form. That improvement and those procedures have moved slowly ahead to the present status of personnel management.

Experiments in Formal Educational Programs

The practitioners and the professors were slow in getting together. The reason was probably that neither side quite trusted the other. In our own experience, the first real, and in some respects most successful, attack on the teaching of personnel management in the universities was engineered in the early 1930's by Samuel C. May of the Department of Political Science at the University of California at Berkeley. Each year for several years, he selected five to ten promising graduate students embarking on the initial work required for a master's degree. He then arranged for them to spend four days a week doing carefully selected types of personnel work at Sacramento, ninety-nine miles away, as members of the technical staff of the central personnel agency of the State of California. One day a week they spent at the university attending a two-hour evening session of a seminar course in personnel management, doing required research, and in some instances attending other classes. At the outset, each of these selected students spent from one to five days working in each of the technical and clerical units of the state personnel agency, observing how operations were carried on, participating in the handling of the personnel transactions, asking questions of the personnel technicians, and learning something of the operating procedures and problems of the several units. After this round of observation, informal instruction, and limited participation in personnel activities, each one of the students was assigned to one of the technical operating units as a learner-doer. Learning was uppermost for a few weeks, but productive work was a hard and fast requirement from the very first day of the work assignment.

During the first semester the students received no cash remuneration but were, each Monday, transported between Sacramento and Berkeley. During the second semester each was paid in cash something less than the usual rate for the lowest professional level for personnel technicians. At the end of the second semester each successful student was given full civil status with regular pay for the work being done. Academically each student was given half the credits required for the master's degree and allowed also, as a part of the work-study activities, to prepare the thesis required for the master's degree.

The joint academic and personnel operating results of this first year of work-study were unusually good. Each year a sizable number of interested and capable personnel technicians were added to the growing staff of the State's central personnel agency and during that year a great amount of technical personnel work was accomplished. For various reasons, not among them that it failed to accomplish useful and desirable results, the plan was discontinued at Berkeley. However, a considerable number of those students entered personnel work in the state and elsewhere and became a part of the growing body of trained and experienced personnel management technicians.

Another type of personnel management training was involved in a plan to develop capable personnel technicians in number. This approach was used first, beginning in 1938, in the personnel unit of the U.S. Department of Labor under Robert C. Smith, and, on a considerably larger scale, beginning in 1942, in the civilian personnel unit of what was then the Air Service Command, under Eldred M. Cocking. Mr. Smith assembled approximately a dozen promising young men and women and gave them group instruction and carefully chosen work assignments, with the two closely coordinated. He managed within a few months to build around the top personnel technicians in the unit a well-rounded technical staff by this means. Mr. Cocking followed substantially the same plan in building up a staff to handle classification, pay, and some budget, recruiting, and organization work in the Air Service Command. There were other similar movements here and there. The above are mentioned as outstanding examples.

Necessary Qualifications of Potential Practitioners

Personnel managers can be trained, and they need that training. The many demonstrations over the years prove that personnel management administrators and technicians can be trained and even the traits and personal characteristics necessary

61

for success in this field can be discovered in prospective trainees, but the universities and colleges followed rather than taking the lead. The large graduate schools of business administration have succeeded in training business administrators, but only incidentally have made direct efforts to train men and women for the public service in personnel administration. There has been a need for such trained personnel and our educational institutions are taking note of this need. But, they should be leading, not following.

In conclusion, it seems in order to point out briefly what has been learned about the selection of those to be taught the science and the art of personnel management. This field is not for the failures, not for those unfit for the service or for industry. The best shall serve the state. The states' work has grown more difficult year after year, more complicated and often dangerous in its methods and presentations. In routine public work and often in other disciplines, a substantial part of the technical personnel work is relatively simple, yet those without intellectual ability cannot cope with the numerous difficult technical and human relations problems that have to be dealt with daily. The ability to use correct English, the ability to communicate, orally and in writing, with others of varied occupational, educational, and social backgrounds are necessities. In short, the public worker needs to be an individual able to communicate to others what he is thinking, recognizing that being a part of the public service he is a part of its image and is always on parade, to be praised, to be condemned or to be ignored. He is not merely another worker—he is a participant. The successful personnel technician, it seems, needs always to have attention directed not to himself or herself but to the personnel problem that must be dealt with and to the personnel principles underlying its successful handling. He is, in a way, a salesman of sound personnel working principles. There is no room in his make-up for intellectual dishonesty and lack of proper loyalty to the organization in which employed, to fellow workers, and to his country.

PART III

THE BASIC TOOLS
OF PERSONNEL MANAGEMENT

Introduction to Part III

The early practitioners of personnel management developed and put into use a considerable number of personnel management working procedures. At the outset, each of these was little more than a practice developed by some resourceful personnel practitioner to enable him to escape the difficulties involved in following precedent or to avoid frequent improvisation. The practices found effective were often copied by others. Slowly numerous personnel management tools were developed, tested, and put to use. Many were embodied in personnel statements; others were contained in reports of personnel management studies that have not been widely publicized. Still others were little more than worthwhile practices used by a few forward-looking personnel practitioners.

This section of the book tries to bring together this body of personnel management knowledge, guides and tools. The information stated herein does not constitute a complete compilation and undoubtedly there are some errors and omissions. Nevertheless it is believed that this statement and explanation of the principal personnel management working procedures and tools may prove interesting to the considerable body of personnel management practitioners we now have and of real value to those trying to learn about the personnel management field.

CHAPTER 13

The Personnel Management Program

At this stage of development of our knowledge of the nature, scope and soundness of the personnel management program and the personnel transactions that occur and recur in establishing, maintaining, changing and discontinuing the employer-employee relationship, there should be little uncertainty about the need for a definite outline of a program to achieve these objectives. Such a program is not a simple matter to formulate. There are broad aspects to be considered. Questions arise, such as: What is administratively feasible? What is effective? What working agreements can be established and maintained? In the earlier parts of this book we have discussed already the guides that have been found to be helpful in deciding on a personnel program and in efforts to implement it.

In both large and small, and private and government, organizations, there must be some form of personnel machinery, meaning the arrangements for achieving the personnel management objectives, determined and stated by the managing officers of the organization. In small business and government organizations, the machinery is likely to be simple and informal. Yet even there arrangements must be made relating to pay, recruiting, work hours and conditions, work assignments, leaves, separations, and other personnel matters. The personnel management machinery problems increase in numbers, diversity and complexity as the number of positions and employees increases. While the statements made apply particularly to the larger organizations, they exist in the smaller organizations and are used in a measure by managing officers.

As a first step in achieving the predetermined personnel objectives, a sound and comprehensive personnel management program is required. The program must meet operating requirements and, when implemented, contribute consistently and substantially to the attainment of the personnel objectives. The program should be comprehensive enough to cover all the personnel management operations directly and indirectly involved in establishing, maintaining, changing and discontinuing the employer-employee relationship. The entire program should be in written form and available to all concerned.

Implementation of the Personnel Management Program

The question of who should have the responsibility for implementing the prescribed program raises some doubts as to the proper and best answer. The managing and administrative officers of business organizations have held to the "foreman personnel autonomy" concept; yet that no longer becomes the best answer. The increasing attention being given to employee rights has raised this question. As the situation presently appears, it seems likely that the place and the authority of the central personnel agency will increase as a defensive barrier to the growing power and persistence of the employees. Without a central personnel agency, or a specific program laid down by the central authority, the execution of any program falls to each supervisory officer; in each jurisdiction one must devise and administer his own personnel system for his operating unit.

In those government organizations that have an active central personnel agency with a professional staff, the picture changes. In nearly all such agencies is one personnel management system for the whole organization. The personnel rules of the agency spell out the role of the administrative officers, individual employees and prospective employees in developing personnel management tools and handling routine personnel transactions.

In any of the variations that may exist, the chief executive of the organization has the ultimate responsibility, both legally and practically, for implementing the personnel program pre-scribed. To function effectively, the central personnel agency must be the authorized agent of the chief executive and, with few exceptions, be directly responsible to him. The personnel agency must be the right hand of the chief executive in personnel matters; with this status the agency's influence extends to other depart-ments and agencies of the government or organization. Acting at the direction of the executive, the central personnel agency advises department heads and their administrative and supervi-sory assistants, employee representatives and other interested parties that this relationship exists and will function as directed.

Role of the Central Personnel Agency

Clothed with the proper authority both by the statutes and executive order, provided with sufficient staff, the agency may proceed to build or add to the personnel management plans and procedures and, further, must assume the responsibility for so doing.

Written rules and regulations must be provided for the use and guidance of the agency itself and for department and agency heads and their administrative officers and supervisory assistants, for employee organizations, if any, and for individuals and spokesmen for them and for others who may be concerned with all personnel transactions. The central personnel agency must also develop certain personnel management tools for handling person-nel transactions to achieve personnel objectives.

In summary, the central personnel agency must establish and maintain working relationships with other participants in the organization. These include the legislative body or the board of directors, the legislative committees, the chief executive, the administrative and supervisory officers in the operating agencies, the employee groups and their representatives, the "housekeep-ing" agencies and officers, and the interested "outside" groups and individuals. Without these or comparable working relation-ships the central personnel agency cannot develop or maintain the effective operation of a sound and comprehensive personnel system.

CHAPTER 14

Personnel Rules and Regulations

Personnel regulations of some kind, dealing with master and servant, director and worker, bondsman and slave, or employer and employee, are as old as history. But only in modern times, in fact almost in our generation, have these relationships been publicly recognized and employee rights been formally included in the negotiations concerning conditions of employment. These relationships have grown in character and complexity until they now involve practically every phase of activity resulting from and in these relationships. New employees, for example, must have ready information on the established procedures of the organization that they must accept and observe. Written personnel regulations help to insure that such matters will be determined carefully and methodically in advance, rather than in the middle of difficult situations.

In this chapter written personnel regulations suitable for a sizable business or government organization are dealt with. Their purpose is to serve as the chief executive's directions and guidance to officers and employees in personnel matters. They specify how transactions may be handled to achieve definite personnel objectives as certainly, easily, and promptly as possible. And, to achieve these ends, these regulations specify, for each type of personnel transaction, who originates it; who participates in it and in what manner; who approves it, modifies it, or disapproves it; and, who, when it has been approved, puts it into effect.

It will be noted that the above is concerned primarily with objectives, procedures and responsibilities. The minute details about means, such as the forms to be used, the affixing of signatures and initials, the number of copies of a document to be prepared, and the like are not usually included in personnel rules.

Suggested Components of Personnel Rules

To be reasonably useful, a set of personnel rules must include:

(a) The name and title of the officer or agency with rule-making power and the date the rules become effective.

(b) A statement of the purpose and application of the rules.

(c) A repetition of any pertinent provisions of the personnel mandates, prescriptions, and authorizations of the managing officers.

(d) A statement of the responsibility for development of each of the personnel management tools, of the principal procedures to be used in developing such tools, of the nature and end products to be produced, and the manner of using these end products in carrying on the personnel management operations.

(e) A statement about who is responsible and the procedures to be used in originating, deciding, implementing, recording, and reporting each type of personnel transaction.

(f) A statement about who is responsible for designing, reproducing, using, filling out, and filing the various forms used in personnel management operations.

(g) Designation of types of personnel records to be kept centrally and of the responsibility for establishing and maintaining such personnel records.

(h) A statement of the procedures to be followed in submitting, preauditing, and certifying payrolls and in reporting personnel irregularities found.

(i) A statement of the extent to which the officers and employees of the organization and members of the public may have access to the central personnel records and of the time and manner in which they may exercise this privilege.

(j) A statement of the extent to which, and the manner in which, departures from the normal personnel transaction procedures may be permitted; provision for recording and reporting any such departures, along with the reasons for them.

(k) A statement of the actions to be taken when the personnel rules are ignored or violated.

(l) A statement of special measures that may be taken when personnel management emergencies occur or when special and unusual personnel needs of a temporary nature arise.

(m) A statement of the manner in which amendments to the personnel rules may be made.

Personnel Tools

In the procedures for handling the personnel transactions to achieve the desired objectives involved, we come back to the development of the personnel tools required. While they will be discussed in some detail later in this book, it seems useful to at least list them here. First of these tools is the position classification plan; based on this are the pay plan, the recruiting plan, the service rating plan, the employee safety and security plan, the separation plan, and others. These personnel tools are meant to facilitate the handling of personnel transactions in accordance with the procedures prescribed. The tools and the procedures are intertwined in so many ways that the personnel regulations are likely to be most useful when the two are dealt with together.

The personnel objectives, the procedures for handling the personnel transactions, and the prescriptions for developing and using the several necessary tools determine for the most part the content and form of the personnel regulations. There are two complicating factors, however, that keep the matter from being simple and without difficulties. The first is that the in-service transactions sometimes involve planning, production, finances, reporting, and other phases of the administrative process to a greater degree than they involve the personnel phases. Experience has shown that matters such as work assignment and items relating thereto should not be included here. These matters fit more naturally in the production domain.

The second factor complicating the procedure is the division of function frequently found in the public service between the board or commission and the personnel director. Where this situation exists, by fiat of the executive or by agreement, the best solution would seem to be two sets of prescriptions: one from the board or commission dealing with the personnel matters with which it is required or desires to concern itself, and one for and by the executive officer dealing with the more numerous matters delegated to him as administrator. There is a great deal of experience showing that when the commissioner or any multiple body undertakes administrative work the results have not been satisfactory. The two divisions in some way should be recognized for the sake of clarity, understanding and administrative results.

As to the personnel objectives to be stated in the personnel regulations, the chief executive or the body authorized to take such action should make clear the policies and procedures that shall govern. First he will want the organization of which he is the executive to be operated by and with a personnel well qualified, well—but not extravagantly—paid, and highly productive and therefore as small as possible in number. Second, to achieve this end, the personnel regulations should include procedures for handling the recruiting, in-service and separation transactions and prescriptions and must provide for the developing and use of the needed personnel tools. The third personnel objective usually stated is that the employees, supervisors, other officers and the central personnel agency are to participate in the handling of the several transactions in the manner indicated in the personnel regulations. The fourth should affirm that it is the duty and the responsibility of each one given a part in the development of personnel tools and in the handling of the personnel transactions to play that part in such a manner as to contribute to the stated objective.

After this statement of purpose must come the meat of the regulations—the description of the procedures and tools, the determination of what is to be prescribed and the form in which it is to be prescribed. While clarity and preciseness are desirable, brevity should not be allowed to prevent the aims from being clearly understood. There needs to be a prescription for every matter, setting forth the normal procedure for handling personnel transactions and specifying how deviations from normal procedures are to be made if circumstances so dictate. These prescriptions should indicate in unmistakable terms: what is to be and the way it is to be done; what is left to the discretion of somebody concerned with a given personnel transaction; and who has the responsibility for originating, passing upon, and recording that transaction. And the technical personnel terms used should be defined, with clarity and exactitude.

In some manner, one by one, the separate personnel regulations must be drafted. They should be arranged in some logical order, such as:

(a) The basic personnel mandates and prescriptions contained in the constitution, charter, articles of incorporation, or partnership agreement, and in the legislation or the actions of the board of directors.

(b) The formal action of the chief executive putting the personnel regulations into effect, including the effective date.

(c) The statement of objectives.

(d) The units dealing with procedures and tools. The material is preferably arranged by subject matter, with those sections relating to recruiting transactions first, those relating to inservice transactions next, and those relating to separation transactions after that. Internal arrangement within any of these groups is substantially the same as in this book.

(e) The regulations delineating the needed personnel machinery, including the establishment and maintenance of certain personnel records; the reporting of personnel events to the central personnel agency and the chief executive; the preaudit and certification of payrolls by the central personnel agency; and the coordinating of operating, financial and personnel operations.

(f) The definition of terms.

Personnel Rules as a Guide

All of these basic personnel operating procedures, mandates and prescriptions serve to lay out what is to be done and for what purpose, to indicate the personnel program, to specify allocation of responsibility, and to set up personnel machinery. But they should not be looked upon as unchangeable. They must not prevent a measure of elasticity based upon the integrity and common sense of the administrator. They are for guidance and may be changed or adjusted. Exactness and workability are the goals. If the prescriptions state that the services of employees are to be appraised periodically, the time should be fixed. If the prescriptions state that an appraisal shall be made of the quality of the work of each employee, the action to be taken following good or poor evaluations should be stated. In other words, these actions should not be mere exercises—they should add something to the quality of the service.

It is not feasible to put down in minute detail procedures for developing personnel tools and handling personnel transactions, however. Instead, the person dealing with a personnel situation needs to have in writing a guide, not law, answering the questions that confront him. The mandates and prescriptions are concerned principally with personnel objectives, with the personnel program, with personnel responsibilities, and with personnel machinery. To some extent they must touch on the specific operating procedures to be used in dealing with specific personnel situations. The administrator will thus be enabled to make intelligent decisions based upon strict guidelines.

CHAPTER 15

The Central Personnel Agency

The responsibility for implementing the personnel management program of business organizations differs widely and in many respects. In many businesses the rank and file employees are hired by departmental officers and their aides or selected in hiring halls where unions have assumed control. In government service the situation is different but not consistent. There are now central personnel agencies in practically all larger governments; yet in the small counties, towns and special districts, much time is still spent in arguing and sometimes feuding over who shall be named constable, clerk or policeman. The old notion of the spoils of victory is still extant.

Importance of the Central Personnel Agency

The central personnel agency is nonetheless here to stay as an integral part of public administration. Its values and uses have been tested. The best governments are those that have a strong personnel agency; the poorest are those without an agency or with one that functions poorly. There are likely to be differences of opinion as to the proper role and functions of an agency, and model civil service statutes by the score have been written by various individual agencies. The situation is complicated by the fact that the central personnel agency is not alone in most of its activities. The employee and the future employee, the employer and his supervisors, and others all have their parts that cannot be neglected or forgotten. It remains true, however, that no sizable government can handle its personnel problems without somebody or some agency skilled in the work that it must perform, anymore than an engineering problem could be dealt with successfully without an engineer.

The central personnel agency thus supplies the skill required for the development, maintenance and proper administration of classifications, pay, recruiting, service plans and other activities in personnel management. It can, or should, coordinate personnel objectives and procedures constructively with production, distribution, service, financial, procurement and other administrative objectives.

In a large public agency or an industrial corporation with hundreds of employees, a central personnel agency can be established to give help in the functions of personnel management. It may be designated as a personnel department, civil service commission, or some other identifying name. Small organizations mostly forego the advantages of the central personnel agency because it costs too much, while the large organization can establish its own personnel unit without prohibitive costs and without undue effort.

It must be remembered that the establishment of such an agency does not assure good or even improved personnel administration. But when properly conceived, organized, manned and administered, the central personnel agency becomes essential and assures personnel results not otherwise attainable.

At a minimum, such an agency would have these objectives and capabilities:

(a)   Makes available within the organization the services of one or more skilled personnel technicians who can give their undivided attention to personnel matters.

(b)   Given a proper personnel assignment, it makes an attack on certain personnel problems advantageously.

76

Among these are the development, maintenance, and proper administration of classification, pay, recruiting, and service rating plans. These require greater technical skills and more extensive authority than the heads of the several operating units possess.

(c) Brings about close coordination of personnel objectives, programs, and procedures with production, distribution, service, financial, procurement, and other administrative objectives, programs, and procedures. Such coordination can never be close or continuous when exercised through numerous unit supervisors or without the skill of a trained personnel administrator or technician.

Right and Wrong Ways To Use the Agency

There are at least three errors often made when establishing and dealing with central personnel agencies. The first, common in government service, is to consider the agency merely the watchdog standing at the gateway lest the professional politicians and political organizations try to place unqualified special interests in positions. The second error, common in business organizations, is to provide the form for a central personnel agency, but to withhold the authority to effectively perform its designated functions. The third error, closely related to the latter and found in both public and private sectors, is to set up a central personnel agency merely to conform to the prevailing personnel fashion and fail to use its latent usefulness.

There are many positive ways in which to effectively use a personnel agency, however. In the preceding pages of this book a serious effort has been made to relate its purposes, proper activities and advantages. To cite again the advantages of a central personnel agency, as the agent of the chief executive, it can:

— Prepare the personnel regulations governing the development and use of the personnel tools and the handling of the recruiting, in-service, and separations transactions in accordance with the statutes and/or the authorization of the chief executive or other appropriate authority.

77

— Take the lead in developing the tools of personnel administration, and to help establish their use in the organization.

— Take the part assigned to the agency in the personnel regulations in handling personnel transactions, and to assist the supervisors and employees in taking their parts. Such assistance is mostly handled by the agency technical staff.

— Keep and maintain the essential personnel records. These records are not trifling things and are vital to an ongoing vigorous agency. They must be currently maintained and available to both supervisory officers and employees alike for reference and procedures thereunder. In considering a proposed pay raise, for example, four of the significant facts needed are the scale of pay established for the class, the present rate of pay of the employee, the length of time he has received that rate, and the appraisal of performance as shown by the service rating of the employee.

— Conduct a preaudit and certification of payrolls before payments for personal services may be made—required in most public jurisdictions. The purpose is to keep track of who has been hired and who is being paid and whether the person hired and listed for payment was hired through proper procedures as required under the statutes. This practice is not common in business organizations and, while there must be a careful recording of who is being hired and who is being paid, it is a matter of business and not of law.

The preaudit and certification of payrolls is a tool of great power and control. Through this method the central personnel agency currently and reliably learns who are employed, and for what periods, under what titles, and at what rates of pay. In a word, the agency arms itself with significant personnel information that is a sure means of obtaining the respectful attention of the department heads and their assistants. This type of control is not always popular with department and agency heads and supervisors and they are likely to consider it a needless bureaucratic procedure to increase costs and hamper their work. Citizens who have not thought the matter through are sometimes in agreement with this feeling.

It is the responsibility of the chief executive, the legislative body or the board of directors to empower the central personnel agency to preaudit and certify the payroll. Without this authority, the agency cannot serve them or the citizens effectively.

— Keep the necessary records for positions classification and payroll. For personnel matters, efficient record-keeping requires two sets of records for each employee: a card on which the salient facts about the employee's service in the organization are shown and an individual file containing all the papers relating to his service. There is a growing use of personnel statistics now even in small organizations. It is always useful to know the number and kinds of positions and employees, the amount of the weekly and annual payroll, and the extent and location of the labor turnover. When this was first written there was an increasing dependence on machine record-keeping and interpretation of such records. Now in practically all large organizations this is common practice and the old method becomes the exception. Personnel records, personnel statistics, and personnel reports are all alike in one fundamental respect—they may be very useful in operating a personnel system or they may be so conceived and maintained that they are not worth the time and energy to produce.

Given its proper function in fashioning the personnel regulations, developing the personnel tools, assisting with the handling of personnel transactions, and in keeping centrally certain essential personnel records, and given the authority needed to carry out these functions effectively, the central personnel agency still has another requirement necessary for it to function efficiently—it must be properly placed within the organization itself.

The properly conceived personnel agency has no basic reason for existence except as it serves the chief executive, helping him handle the personnel transactions in an orderly and effective fashion. It cannot be emphasized too often that the central personnel agency belongs in the chief executive establishment regardless of where and how it receives its departmental funds. The agency cannot take any important part in the handling of personnel transactions as long as it gives first priority to policing the units concerned and does no other productive work in the administration. The place of the personnel agency is at the right hand of the executive.

Basic Factors for Effective Central Personnel Agencies

It cannot be said that there is but one method of dealing with personnel problems regardless of all attending circumstances, of course, but there are a few guiding principles.

The headquarters central personnel agency, as the agent of the chief executive, in accordance with his prescriptions and with his approval, should prescribe personnel objectives and policies for each local unit. The central agency must prescribe regulations setting forth procedures to be used in handling personnel transactions and must establish classification, pay, recruiting, service rating, employee safety and security, separation, and other plans. In addition, the headquarters personnel technicians should from time to time visit the local personnel units, note conditions and operations, answer questions, and give advice or voice admonitions that the local personnel people should be free to accept or reject. While the local personnel unit should be autonomous as far as the headquarters personnel unit is concerned, the local personnel director must be responsible to the officer in charge of the local operations.

CHAPTER 16

The Position Classification Plan

The position classification plan is one of the marked successes in the development of the science and art of personnel management. The concepts and procedures needed for the development, maintenance, and effective use of this basic personnel tool are known. Again and again, in actual practice, the personnel practitioners have successfully used position classification plans to achieve their personnel objectives. It is at the base of the success of personnel management and thoroughly established as such.

For emphasis it seems advisable to repeat the significant facts involved. First, as the term "position classification" itself indicates, the classification is of positions and not of persons; the incumbent of any position that is classified, for all personnel management purposes and for most work purposes, automatically takes the title of the position held. It is the position, not the incumbent, that is classified. Second, the classification plan, of itself, achieves no personnel management objectives. It is a means of achieving desired personnel management ends and not an end in itself. Third, in any sizable organization only the crudest types of personnel management work are possible without this basic personnel tool.

A good position classification plan has two outstanding virtues. In the first place, it reduces to manageable proportions the thousands of facts about positions, and to some degree about employees, that otherwise can overwhelm the managing officers, and personnel technicians, and anybody in an organization who is concerned with more than one or two operating units. Secondly, it is the master tool used in building most of the other tools and in carrying on day-to-day personnel management operations. Therefore, these two factors make it possible to assert, rather dogmatically, that in any organization of considerable size there can be no very high type of personnel administration until a good position classification plan is constructed, adopted, and put to its appointed uses.

Elements of a Position Classification Plan

The primary objective in developing the position classification plan for all or designated positions in any good-sized government, business, or other organization is to group those positions, which are inevitably diverse in nature and which may be scattered among numerous operating and geographical units, into homogeneous classes. Each class includes all the positions in the whole organization that are so much alike in duties, responsibilities, organization relationships, and other significant characteristics that they may be treated alike in the handling of the pay, recruiting, in-service, separation, and other personnel management operations. When completed, these class specifications would consist of the following parts:

(a) The title of the class;

(b) The definition of the class;

(c) The statement of typical tasks performed by those holding positions allocated to the class or a description of the typical positions allocated to the class;

(d) A statement of the knowledge, abilities, skills, and personal attributes generally believed or known to be necessary for the successful and satisfactory performance of the tasks;

(e) A statement of the objective evidence believed or known to indicate the possession of one or more of the needed knowledges, abilities, skills, and personal attributes;

(f) A statement of the principal or usual lines of promotion to and from the class; and

(g) The adopted flat or graduated rate of pay for the class.

Whether these items are listed separately or combined, they need to be recognized and used.

Data Sources for Classification

When a new classification is to be made or an existing one is to be overhauled or renovated, the information needed for classification purposes can be best obtained from these three principal sources:

(a) The formal and informal work assignments that have been given the several operating units; and their annual and special reports dealing with their internal organization, their operating procedures, their staffing, their accomplishments, their current problems, and their plans and needs;

(b) The written statements of the individual officers and employees, each on a carefully designed position description form, describing the tasks performed, the responsibilities exercised, and the work relationships, all revised and supplemented to the extent necessary but not alerted by the immediate supervisors and by the department head or his designated representatives;

(c) The personnel observations made by members of the classification staff and the information gained in discussions with the department heads, with their administrative and supervisory assistants, and with the individual officers and employees.

All these data can be and are collected in other ways usually designed to save time and energy. Time and the best informed workers in the field, however, have demonstrated that none of these so-called time-saving plans produce information complete and accurate enough to produce satisfactory results. Thoroughness and correctness are the two guide posts in the whole process.

Classification experience shows quite conclusively that the information about the individual positions and their incumbents is most accurate, most complete, and most usable for classification purposes when the incumbent of each position records on a specially designed position-description-form the factual information requested. The recorded form is then reviewed and, to the extent necessary, supplemented and certified as correct and reasonably complete by the immediate superior and then by the department head or his designated representative. These three persons are best informed about what the facts asked for really are and are generally willing to take the time to record what they know. The position descriptions thus obtained constitute the working bible of the classification technicians.

Steps in Classifying Positions

When the needed information has been ascertained and recorded, the classification technicians are able to decide, at least tentatively, upon the classes of positions to be recognized, the title to be given to each class recognized, and the allocation of the individual positions to the appropriate classes. Supplemented by field observations and conferences with officers and employees, the technicians can confirm, amend, and change their tentative classifications if and when necessary. Many positions ''classify themselves,'' but the tentative classification of many other positions calls for technical insight and competence, judgment, and conferences with the operating officers and others. This is true particularly when considering dividing lines between the classes in a series and many of the titles and allocations.

When the matter of titles is settled at any time some class definitions may be written and made ready for final reviews and editing. Other class definitions, where lines are finely drawn, cannot be prepared until the recorded information has been analyzed and decisions made as to the classes that are to be recognized.

In writing a class specification, the proper order has been found to be: the title, next the definition of the class expressed entirely in terms of work done and responsibilities exercised. Next are illustrations of the class, which may take the form of examples of typical tasks or a description of one or more positions allocated to the class. Next follows the listing of the knowledge, skills, abilities, and personal attributes believed to be necessary and desirable for the efficient performance of the work that has been defined and described. Sometimes this listing is divided: first, the things to be required; second, additional things considered desirable even though they are not required specifically. A few practitioners think that good specifications also must include data showing the number, the department, and the geographical location of the positions allocated to the class and a succinct statement of their place in the organization. This may be done but in our opinion it is not essential.

It must be remembered, however, that the class definition is the most vital part in classification work. Without correct definitions and specifications, neither the administrator, his assistants nor even the department authorities can make correct decisions as to classes, titles, and allocations.

When the classification plan is completed by the classifiers, the next step is a final review by departmental officers and supervisors. It is not their function to write the specifications. It is, however, their right and their obligation to satisfy themselves that they are right and present their own opinions, approval or disapproval thereof. Agreement having been reached, or at least all differences having been given careful consideration, the classifying agency prepares its proposed and formal report containing classes, titles and allocations. For the sake of clarity, the classifier should make an explanation of the manner in which the classification work has been carried on; the proposals respecting classes, titles and allocations; a statement of the differences between the classification staff and the operating officers, if any; definite plans for review and adoption of the proposals, with or without modification; and the steps that should be taken in implementing, using, maintaining, and amending the adopted classification plan. All of these items are of importance because a classification plan or any plan affecting large numbers of people can never be considered as a fixed product. Changes are constantly being made in the internal organization, the operating procedures, the work program, and the staffing of the organization, and in work assignments of individual officers and employees, responsibilities, and organization relationships of existing positions. To keep it current it requires constant watching and frequent amendments.

Uses of the Position Classification Plan

In portraying, rather broadly, the methods of fashioning, adopting, and maintaining the position classification plan, it has been repeatedly emphasized that it is the master personnel tool. It is used, along with the personnel assignment and the personnel regulations, in constructing and using the plans for the cited purposes. No matter how soundly conceived, fashioned and maintained, it has no value unless it is used for the proper personnel purposes for which it was designed and made. As stated earlier, in practice, the class specifications serve at least four purposes. First, and most important, they are essential for recruiting purposes. Second, they serve as proof that such a plan is maintained and that effective personnel administration is carried out. Third, for the personnel consulting organization, the quality of the class specifications may be used as a powerful selling document when classification work is needed or sought. And fourth, the plan constitutes a means of recording classification decisions.

The entire position classification plan, encompassing the class specifications, as has been said, is the master personnel tool. Not only does it provide a means whereby masses of information may be concisely handled, it also supplies a base from which all other personnel plans and tools derive.

CHAPTER 17

The Pay Plan

Once the position classification plan has been established, it is possible to attack with assurance and equity any of the numerous, remaining personnel problems. When the nature of each position is known in detail and the positions have been grouped into homogeneous classes and given short descriptive titles, when to each class has been allocated all the positions in the organization so much alike in duties, responsibilities, and other characteristics that they may be treated alike for pay, recruiting, and other personnel purposes, then the matter of pay may be attacked with some assurance.

Pay matters are always controversial and certainly as controversial as any other part of the whole personnel management field. The first personnel problems are likely to occur in the area of pay. In most organizations pay and pay levels take more time than any other problem involved in personnel services. No pay plan can be considered final or permanent and no one pay plan suits everybody. Economic and employment conditions as they exist today create the need for pay changes. It is natural for employees to want higher pay rates and higher earnings than they are receiving. All in all, it is difficult in any business or government to ignore pay matters for any lengthy period.

Responsibility for Establishing the Pay Plan

Achieving the objective of a personnel well paid, but not extravagantly so, is no easy matter. The managing officers of the organization, the financial officers, the central personnel agency, and the representatives of the employees all have important parts to play. Unfortunately the financial officers, as a rule, decline to take any effective part in working out pay policies, levels, rates, and scales. The employee representatives, when properly encouraged, generally assist effectively. However, they make pay problems more difficult by insisting that an undue proportion of all available funds be used for personnel services or by fighting to get preferential treatment for the groups they represent. In any case, the central personnel agency, if properly organized and administered, is likely to take the lead in collecting and analyzing the pay, cost-of-living, and other pertinent data needed by the managing officers in their efforts to arrive at a pay plan.

In all of this, the managing officers make the final decisions upon pay policies that, when implemented, should give practical effect to the principle of relating pay closely to the work done. In accordance with the policies determined by the managing officers about pay levels, the use of flat rates or scales of pay, conformity with or departures from community and trade pay practices, and other pay matters, the central personnel agency, assisted as far as may be by the financial officers and representatives of employee groups, must have a part in the pay plan and pay regulations.

Factual Information Needed for Pay Plan

No matter who takes the initiative in pay-plan matters, four different types of factual information are needed when attention is seriously given to pay conditions. The first information needed is the amount of the payroll in dollars and cents for the current payroll period, for the last fiscal or calendar year, for a series of previous years, and the relation of the total payroll to total operating expenditures. The second set of facts represents a partial breakdown of the first: the rates or scales of pay for some or all of the larger classes making up approximately half of the total work force. The third set of facts requires considerable but not exhaustive data about the pay situation in the community and in the trade in general, without regard to geographic location. As a rule, community pay practices are more significant than trade or industry practices, but data on both are desirable. The fourth set of facts has to do with the relationships among the rates or scales of pay within the organization.

This is the guiding principle to which all the information should be applied: At the levels determined by the financial resources and policies of the employer, pay should be related as closely as possible to the work done. This is a policy of perfection, happening rarely, but it does require some straight thinking and the use of a number of financial and personnel devices.

Setting Pay-Plan Limits

First of all, the employer must determine what his financial resources are as they affect the amount he sets aside for pay for personal services. The upper pay limit is clearly the employer's ability to expend his intake and capital for that purpose. Neither the employer nor his employees benefit when this upper limit is exceeded. In business organizations, exceeding it except for short periods of time means financial embarrassment, at times temporary closing of plants, sometimes permanent closing. In government organizations, exceeding this limit, except for short periods, can mean enforced furloughs without pay or doubtful financial practices that may end in a political turnover.

The lower limit for pay rates and earnings is fixed on the basis of the amount required to attract sufficient workers in the lower classes. The upper limit involves not only the rate required to attract workers but frequently involves personal or group interest and influence. The upper limit represents the ability and willingness of the employer to pay. The lower level represents the lowest rates that, with the recruiting methods in effect, attract qualified workers in the numbers needed over a period of months and years.

Deciding upon the exact amount to be reserved for wages and salaries in any fiscal year is not a simple matter in either a business or a government organization. There is some leeway possible in allocating available funds, but there is always a maximum that may not be exceeded in either the short run or the long run. Pay decisions should always be made in relation to the overriding principle that the pay of the employee is closely related to the kind and quality of work he is doing and the proficiency with which he is doing it.

CHAPTER 18

Recruiting, Induction and In-Service Training Plans

The recruiting of prospective qualified employees in both government and industry is as important as it is difficult, and to assume that we know and practice a standard procedure that will produce the desired results is evidence that expectations are far removed from facts. The industrial world follows many procedures; some follow the foreman-hiring idea, others have elaborately organized central personnel agencies maintained at high costs, but only a small proportion of these follow the best known scientific or businesslike procedures.

As this book is particularly designed for use in public administration, the emphasis is on what the writer considers the best practices in the field of public personnel management. It should be said at the beginning, although it is likely to be disputed by personnel managers in business, that all the best and most effective practices in the personnel procurement and maintenance field are not in the nongovernment field; they are rather in the public service. It is true that disciplinary measures and necessary modifications are accomplished more quickly in industry, service agencies and businesses, but there is sufficient evidence to indicate that changes in numbers of employees in the public service can, have been, and are being made when there is a necessity for such action.

Labor Turnover

Yet, in both the private and public sectors, the labor turnover caused by inefficiency is more than it should be in what we used to call the test or trial period. Labor turnover is expensive both in its cost and in the eventual level of service rendered, and now even the procedures involved may be long drawn out and expensive. Turnover is not the whole story, moreover. Why is the employee-employer relationship often dissolved, or, perhaps worse, continued though one or both of the parties involved are not satisfied? And why do the employers in need of a good employee and the employee in need of a good employer part company after a brief trial period? Conversely, how are changes avoided by the nucleus of employees who remain with the same organization year after year? Until such questions are answered it is not possible to build a sound recruiting plan.

Lack of Standard Tests for Prospective Employees

It is relatively easy for the prospective employer, using the application form, the interview, the investigation, and selected tests, to find out some things about the prospective employee, such as age, sex, weight, height, place of residence, educational attainments, employment history, and other personal data that may or may not be significant. Through the use of properly selected tests, he may discover facts about areas of knowledge, skills, abilities, some personal attributes, some aptitudes, physical condition, strength, and other things that may or may not be significant. Through the interview and investigations, he may learn something about the prospective employee's attitudes, work habits, dress, poise, standing in the community, speech, and other things that, once more, may or may not have significance. The difficulty comes in interpreting the meaning of the data.

Despite the progress made in so many fields of human activity, it must be admitted by every experienced administrator that we have no standard testing procedures that will select qualified prospective employees. The remedy of reformers a century ago was written tests, a step forward and yet a permanent part of employee selection, but what we should now be considering is a whole test made up of the several parts that make it complete and having dependable predictive value. And that, except for few cases, is far in the future. The number of classified positions in the federal service alone is now over eighteen hundred and while we talk hopefully of validated tests, it cannot be proved that more than a hundred of all of these working places and positions do have validated tests that can and will produce the end results that are sought. Such tests require years to complete.

Progress has been made and is being made, but the process is slow. Ways have been developed to test for traits or characteristics with a high validity—an important discovery but these tests may not be used as the whole, well-rounded product. We come back to the fact that the claims for validated tests for many types of work and responsibilities by individuals and associations of various specialties, or a guarantee of results, are not to be accepted.

In the 1920's, and we are not doing a great deal better yet, improvement was made in test construction and testing procedures, relating tasks to the work involved in many classes. The parts or factors in the tests, the weight given to each part, were worked out and tests were made seemingly pertinent. Our tests do eliminate those who lack basic knowledge and skill, but with all these efforts, they did not extend much further.

Recruiting Methods and Devices

The search goes on as it must and here and there interesting projects come to light. There have been some notable successes in the selection process, most clearly the plan drawn up by the Chief of Police of Berkeley, California, who developed a plan for the selection of policemen in the 1920's. He set forth succinctly the qualities and qualifications he wanted and saw possible in recruits for his force in a book he authored. He brought the family into the picture on the theory that the family life of an officer would be affected by the conditions and hours of work. The result was the most effective and most intelligent police force in the country.

Within the limitations of the recruiting process, the competent recruiting technician can use as his guides, not only the objective of a personnel well qualified but also these governing requirements: The recruiting procedures must meet legal requirements; they must comply with the adopted personnel regulations, with the personnel legislation in the public service or the actions of the board of directors; in the business organization, with any constitutional or charter requirements of the organization, and with any pertinent provisions in the law of the land. The recruiting procedures must, as far as is feasible, be appealing to those who participate in the recruiting process—to the prospective employee, to the prospective employer, and to those who represent them in carrying on recruiting operations. The recruiting procedures must be such as to be defensible when questions are raised. And, the recruiting procedures must be the best quality, which will hopefully predict occupational success.

Induction Procedures

The induction of a new employee to and into a working force is an important incident to him and is likewise the same to the employer. Some organizations take care in seeing that the induction process is given its proper emphasis. Others pay little attention to the matter and the new employee is left to find out for himself his place and his part in the working force and his relations with his fellow workers.

In small organizations the capable worker has little difficulty in finding his place and adjusting himself to it. In organizations with several hundred positions or more, handbooks or explanatory literature are often provided, some informal training is given and the employee is assigned to an experienced worker. Some organizations' training departments provide formal training courses that the new employee must attend. Whatever the attention paid to the new employee or the form of training provided, there are real values to starting a new employee in the right way other than increasing the chance that he will do his job well and be happy in his work. That attention gives him confidence and serves also to make him feel that he is being treated as a person in whom the new organization has a human as well as a dollars-and-cents interest.

In-Service Training Plans

In-service training operations are a part of the same process of making the employee a part of the agency or organization and of increasing his capacity to the highest possible level—or at least making him a satisfactory employee. It has long been known that for the most part in-service training is needed at the outset of employment. The required instruction must come from his supervisor or by skilled instructors in formal training courses.

To the extent that it is to be effective, the in-service training plan must be built about the supervisors at the head of the smallest operating units. They are in a better position than anyone else to know training needs, to determine the content and length of the training courses, to select those to be trained, to find suitable instructors, and to cope with other problems. It is possible to conduct in-service training courses for groups, but these must be preceded by the development, adoption, and installation of position classification, pay, and recruiting plans. The group to be trained must be homogeneous in abilities, subject matter, and needs, and the preceding personnel steps will be necessary to insure this homogeneity.

It is pointless to attempt the impossible by choosing ill-suited students or teachers for training courses. It is nonsense to hope that every apprentice can become a good occupation teacher, or to think that the central personnel agency can give worthwhile training courses on the basis of theory and not experience, or to permit enthusiasm to run away with judgment and need so that technical courses beyond the capacity of the worker are undertaken. Under such conditions, the in-service training needs are not being satisfied.

The operating officers must mostly originate, plan, and execute group training courses with the training technician from the central personnel agency having only a minor part therein. Business and government organizations should not undertake to duplicate vocational training or other courses given by educational organizations. The training objective should be to aid the supervisors and supplement their training work. Unless very low in-service training standards are acceptable to the managing officers, training courses for foremen and other supervisors are all but essential. Such courses should be undertaken with the full realization that supervisors, though they have supervisory responsibilities in common, are not likely to be a homogeneous group and the training provided through such courses must be partial and to a degree superficial except as smaller and smaller groups with common work problems are assembled. In any case, those holding positions above the supervisors in charge of the smallest operating units must do a good deal of individual training work with these supervisors if they, in turn, are to be effective teachers in their own right.

Recruiting, induction and in-service training, if directed to the common purpose of making the new employee a part of the organization, will go a long way toward achieving the personnel goals of the organization.

CHAPTER 19

Performance Rating

Without reliable performance ratings, there is no available criterion by which to judge the results of the occupational success tests. And, without knowing how valid these tests are, supervisors are obliged to rate the performance of an employee relying upon tests with "face" validity instead of an actual or proved validity. A long and difficult process must be followed to validate tests in fact and not merely in theory. Here again we have learned how to prepare and administer tests that will measure certain traits and characteristics, but to put all of this essential information together and produce a test that will measure the person in his or her prospective performance in the position is another matter. As mentioned earlier, of the some eighteen hundred classifications of positions in the federal service, we estimate that there are little more than a hundred tests that could be designated as validated, and some of these tests have not been carried through to the performance stage long enough to satisfy scientifically validated requirements.

Work is being done in this field and the tests are being improved, but we can claim only progress. It is a never ending effort just to keep abreast of the changing times and needs of the selective process in government and out. We think it can be said that neither business nor government has solved this problem but that both are seeking the solution. We think we can say further that the recruiting agency and the supervisors have not yet been able or willing to work together as a team. The recruiter feels that he must go on with his task and the supervisor shrinks from the dull and unpopular talk of even requiring high-level performance, let alone recording and using it as a basis of reward or discipline.

Past Achievement in Performance Rating Techniques

Historically these aspects of personnel management have not been entirely neglected. As pointed out above, the fundamental service rating concepts were first worked out and stated by the personnel men in Chicago in the years following 1910. They appear in the rules of the Chicago Civil Service Commission, which are included in its report for the year 1913. The department heads were required to set up standards, maintain written comparative records, and report to the personnel agency the rating made at periodic intervals. The governing rules prescribed further that the recorded ratings should be used as the principal factor in making upward or downward pay adjustments, promotions, layoffs when required, separation from the service and the other disciplinary actions. That was an ambitious program and well worthwhile, but, unfortunately, the plan failed in Chicago and elsewhere it was tried because the raters concentrated on people rather than performance. And even today, though performance ratings are required, they are, as a rule, not well done and they are not likely to be consistent or have a significant relation to the actual performance and conduct of those who are being observed and rated.

Another significant attempt to create a new plan of performance and conduct rating was made by J. B. Probst, then personnel director for St. Paul, Minnesota. About 1925 he began to analyze the problems, discarding the prevailing premises about how performance ratings might be obtained. Probst prepared an elaborate system of performance and conduct reports and devised a scoring plan, to be operated centrally, for translating these reports into ratings. The main findings of the Probst plan are summarized below.

(a) Most supervisors are unable to rate their employees. Supervisors usually remain constant in their opinion of the best and the poorest employee in the group, but agree with their own ratings of individual employees only about fifty percent of the time.

(b) Rating forms must use terms and expressions that the supervisor would ordinarily use in describing his workers. It does not work to ask a supervisor to translate his knowledge of a given worker's performance into a numerical score or to make a generalized report on broad traits.

(c) Supervisors, not high officers, must report on the employee. When more than one supervisor reports on one employee, investigations showed that all should report on the same sheet, the lowest ranking supervisor being the first to do so.

(d) There are at least a hundred elements entering into work success that a supervisor must report on. The significant elements of work success vary from one class of positions to another, although a relatively large number of these items remain the same.

(e) Supervisors must not be allowed to evaluate their own reports because they get distracted from the task of reporting the facts of performance and conduct and generally set out to produce predetermined ratings. Probst evolved his scoring plan by obtaining numerous estimates of occupational success for groups whose supervisors were interested, analytical, and above the average in competence, and then assigning such values to the individual items reported as would produce rankings based on total scores corresponding to the rankings made by the supervisors. There were serious defects to this plan, but the underlying concepts and the experimental procedures are basically sound.

(f) The employee must be informed in some detail of the report on his performance and conduct and of the rating based upon it.

Current Research on Performance Rating

Later research in the field has shown that Probst laid a firm foundation, even while more aspects of the total process are being discovered. The number of work elements entering into and contributing to occupational success is very much larger than administrators anticipated. It has also been found that there needs to be some kind of scale whereby the supervisor can indicate the degree to which a given work element is applicable for a given employee. It is possible to get reasonably accurate reports of performance and conduct unless the supervisor is given the opportunity to report the average degree. It has also been found that more attention must be paid to the selection and training of the supervisors who will ultimately make the reports. The fact remains that the problem of service ratings is yet unsolved.

CHAPTER 20

Safety, Benefit and Separation Plans

In both the public service and in much of the industrial world, concern with the conditions of employment do not end with the signing of a contract between employer and employee. The areas of safety, vacation, sick leave, other leaves with or without pay, contributions by employer and employee to pension or retirement funds, and safeguards of employment are not commonplace in the personnel world. Even these precautions are not insurance against strikes, layoffs, lockouts, resignations and retirements. All of these events must be prepared for in advance.

Workers these days are conscious of the need for safety in their working areas and environment and frequently include this matter as an important factor in their bargaining procedures. They want security also in their employment. The managers and the industrialists have the same interests, both as people interested in their fellowmen and because they know that satisfied workers are an important part of successful business whether many or few workers are employed. In the end, sound administrative principles are not unlike sound social principles.

The first rule of thumb must of course be that the workers are productive. No business or service can be healthy or can last unless the workers produce enough goods or services that can be sold in enough markets to pay them and to maintain the business or industry. The second fact is that the employee, through his own efforts, or with the help of his employer, cannot eliminate or remove all the hazards of his employment. It is a part of his job, however, to minimize the occupational hazards surrounding him, and it is to the management's obvious benefit to assist in all ways. Here again, the interests of the industry, managers, and employees are the same even though arrived at from different points of view.

In any situation where the employer has an essential part in the recruiting, in-service relations and separation transactions, and all of these relationships are always present, there then needs to be some effective means for his participation in them. There must be a general plan of procedure clearly and precisely stated and written down of every step of the way for the information and observance of both sides of the contract.

Basic Elements of Safety and Benefit Plans

There are a bewildering variety of safety rules and regulations stated in the statutes. These rules differ in particulars and procedures so much that, in approaching the problem of devising effective plans, it would seem to be best to begin as if the fields were clear and nothing of importance had been done. In some respects, an employer is free to do as much as he pleases. He may, for example, do about as he likes in handling annual and sick leaves, except in some government organizations where such matters are governed by law or by ordinance. On the other hand, the employer is required to comply with the law as far as the national Social Security and Employment Acts apply to the positions in his organization, although he may of his own volition go beyond them. Safety plans now require provision for injuries and occupational diseases, by forethought and on-the-spot aid all the way through to the payments to employees permanently or temporarily disabled by injuries.

Separation Plan

The presence of the separation process in the employee plan is a somewhat new occurrence. In the past this was given little attention. The employee was fired (dismissed) for cause or left his employment voluntarily and the incident was closed.

102

Under present conditions, when the authority of the employer is often limited, the matter becomes one of major importance.

In separations of all kinds, voluntary or forced, consideration must be given to obligations by the employer and employee. The latter can no longer end the matter by voluntarily resigning. He may have vested rights in his employment, accumulated leave of various kinds, overtime for which payment has not been made in cash or extra paid vacation, and eligibility for retirement or pension plans.

The employer has all of these considerations and some others. He must satisfy all the rights accorded to the employer under union or voluntary arrangements. He must satisfy the unions that the employee has not been forced out, or, if so, that seniority rights have not been violated. He must fill the occurring vacancy. He must maintain a record of the transaction and whether, under all the circumstances involved, the employee should be reemployed. The object of this, and all other such plans, is to insure fair dealing all around.

CHAPTER 21

Summation

EDITORS' NOTE:

As editor, we have felt obliged to rewrite, and sometimes omit, a great deal of Telford's manuscript, but at every step of the way our primary effort has been to eliminate only those parts of it not required to present the basic procedures of personnel management and to record the story he has tried to tell. In a final chapter, Telford undertook to sum up his ideas and something of his philosophy of the whole matter. He speaks personally in this chapter, and while we have consolidated his thinking into fewer words, this summary, as nearly as is possible, is in his own words.

It should be noted that in many places he gets away from "principles" in the strict sense of the word and discusses reason, procedures, causes and suggested remedies, which are not principles. Here he is talking to trainees, interested citizens, politicians and all who may be interested in these processes and procedures, and gives his own philosophy on all these relationships. These items will show all through the text. Here he is the teacher talking to the uninformed.

Charles P. Messick
William W. Boyer

The personnel assignment, the establishment, the delineation and identification of positions; the central personnel agency; the personnel regulations; the manuals of personnel operating procedures; the position classification plan; the performance rating plan—these, in my judgment, are the principal parts of personnel management. There are established procedures and tools by which and with which we classify and develop them. These tools are known, recognized and, most significantly, used in handling recurring personnel transactions. There are, of course, additional matters such as, for example, work assignments and suitable working conditions, but I consider them part of the broad field of administration rather than an aspect of personnel administration.

Some who claim knowledge in this area relegate one or another of these personnel tools to a minor or secondary category. More significantly, perhaps, others would make a number of additions to this list. In particular, some who concern themselves with personnel management would place great stress on employee relations, labor relations, public relations, morale, incentives, grievances, and welfare activities. Others might possibly make these matters the very essence of personnel management. There are omissions in these concepts in my thinking. As to welfare activities, my belief is that welfare work in a business organization is likely to take the form of employer benevolence, paternalism or totalitarianism—all poor substitutes for those things necessarily involved in being a good employer. In emergencies, such as helping employees to find appropriate housing or in extreme cases seeing that their families have food, temporary action may be necessary, but I look with suspicion on any welfare plan for employees that does for the employee what he can and should normally do for himself.

This philosophy has no element of indifference or hard dealing. I believe that the employee and the employer both have some privileges that belong to them. For example, the employee should never lose his right to choose his own job or leave it and take another; the employer must maintain the right to release employees for good reasons when he finds it necessary or required. But problems of employee relations and morale are human problems and as such will arise at any and all stages of the personnel transactions. They can best be dealt with in connection with the standard personnel operations and tools, such as the position classification plan or the pay plan. In the same vein, the

106

best manner for dealing with personnel grievances is to so handle personnel transactions that they do not arise. If a grievance should nonetheless occur, the most effective means of dealing with it is through the personnel transaction that produced it.

I have seen in many organizations, both civilian and military, deliberate steps taken to produce high morale or to produce the opposite result—to prevent low morale. I have tried to separate plans and procedures for dealing with employee relations, labor relations, public relations, morale, incentives and grievances not because I consider these things unimportant in personnel management. I acknowledge that each and all of them are significant. But, first these things do not seem to me to be personnel transactions per se or the tools with which they are accomplished. I look upon them as, to a large extent, escapist devices used by those unwilling to face personnel realities, such as the need to prepare personnel rules or regulations, or to group positions into homogeneous classes and establish for each class of positions rates of pay that relate to the work done, or to cope with research and operating problems involved in recruiting and in establishing reliable service ratings. The concept of employee relations or morale or grievances seem to me to cloud straight personnel thinking without contributing much, if anything, worthwhile to the effectiveness of personnel operations. Finally, I think the end product that all of these terms are intended to produce can be brought about most certainly, most quickly, and most effectively by a wholly different approach.

That better approach, I believe, is the construction and competent use of the several tools and procedures I have described in this book. The personnel administrator and the technician, grounded in the science and skilled in the art of personnel management, along with or as the agent of the managing officers, must set the objectives, build the personnel machinery, determine the broad procedures, develop or adjust the personnel tools and perform the work involved. They must take the lead in devising and using:

    (a)   The pay plan, containing rates or scales of pay for each recognized class of positions, relating pay closely to the work done and assuring for each person employed good but not extravagant pay.

107

(b) The recruiting plan, intended to produce a well-qualified personnel.

(c) The induction and in-service training plans, intended to help in making the employees into understanding, intelligently cooperative and productive workers.

(d) The performance rating plan, intended to measure the total worth of the employee in the organization.

(e) The employee safety and security plan, intended to assure, as far as possible, worker satisfaction, employee safety while at work, and some degree of financial protection in case of injury, inability to work, or unemployment.

(f) The preaudit and certification of payrolls, if authorized by the managing officers, intended to keep the personnel technicians reliably and currently informed of personnel events.

(g) The maintenance of whatever personnel records, statistics and reports as are useful and/or required by law and administrative edict.

These responsibilities are not easy tasks. Many who look at the restrictive personnel tools in business, and especially in government where a driving force is most needed, are critical and question both the need and their usefulness. The argument for these controls is ready and strong. Take away any one of the tools I mentioned and you hamper the personnel technician. Take away the adequate personnel assignment, the personnel regulations, or the position classification plan and you destroy the product you seek to the extent that you deny the authority. Give the competent administrator the personnel tools he requires and the opportunity to use them effectively and the gates are opened to the promised land of good business management and good government.

PART IV

GLOSSARY OF THE
PRINCIPAL TECHNICAL TERMS
USED IN PUBLIC
PERSONNEL ADMINISTRATION

ART: The methods and practices based upon a science that, when consistently used, give reasonable assurance of successful practice in a selected field. *See* PERSONNEL MANAGEMENT, ART OF

CLASS or CLASS OF POSITIONS: A group of positions including all in the organization or in designated portions thereof that are so much alike as to duties, responsibilities, organization relationships and other significant characteristics that they can be treated alike for pay, recruiting, training, employee rating, separation, and other personnel purposes. The grouping of the individual positions into homogeneous classes takes no account of their departmental or geographical location except as they may require significant differences in pay, recruiting, and other personnel operations. Class does not always mean or infer a group. In a large organization there may be only one position in a specific class, especially at the higher levels; for example, chief of police, administrator, purchasing agent.

CLASS DEFINITION: A brief statement, normally in terms of the duties performed, the responsibilities exercised, and the organization relationships existing, indicating with a high degree of accuracy what positions are to be included in and excluded from a given class of positions. The class definition normally includes some such saving clause as "and does other work as required" to take care of the occasional work assignments not related to the regular work. Definitions should not be stated in terms of the qualifications required of the present or future incumbents of the positions allocated to the class.

CLASSES, SERIES OF: Two or more classes of differing levels of difficulty included in the same occupational group, such as *plumber helper, plumber, plumber foreman;* or, *clerk 1* (i.e. beginner), *clerk 2, clerk 3;* or *junior engineer, assistant engineer, associate engineer, senior engineer.*

CLASS TITLE: The name or title given to any recognized class of positions. Examples: *public health nurse, garage serviceman, X-ray technician.* Class titles, as far as possible, should be short, describe or suggest the tasks performed, indicate the level of the class if it is one of a series, and be in accord with the organization and trade class naming practices.

110

DEMOTION: The moving of an officer or employee from one position to another of a lower level, as indicated by a lower flat or maximum rate of pay. A demotion, as thus defined, does not necessarily mean an immediate decrease in the pay of the officer or employee demoted; there may be no change in pay when the graduated scales of pay for the two classes of positions overlap.

ELIGIBLE, APPOINTMENT: The steps taken by the appointing authority to place in a vacant position a person who has been certified to him by the central personnel agency as being eligible for such appointment.

ELIGIBLE, CERTIFICATION: The official certification of the central personnel agency to the appointing authority that a specified person therein may legally be appointed to a vacant position in a specified class of positions. As a rule in the public service, the names of more than one eligible are certified, usually three, sometimes more, and the appointing authority may legally make his selection from those named as the statute or rule prescribes.

ELIGIBLE, EMPLOYMENT: Any person whose name has been placed on the employment list for a specific class of positions.

EMPLOYEE PERFORMANCE REPORT: A written report, by the immediate supervisor or supervisors of an officer or employee, of the significant facts about his performance and conduct during a specified period of time. The supervisor or supervisors making the performance report are those who supervise and direct the employee's work and who know the facts as to his performance and conduct. When there is more than one supervisor, each supervisor makes his own individual report on the same form.

EMPLOYEE RATING: A formal or informal appraisal of the work performance and the conduct, during a specified period of time, of an officer or employee, expressed in numerical, adjective, or other prescribed form. The time period covered by ratings is usually three months, six months or a year, although the periods may vary.

EMPLOYEE RATING PLAN: The prescription of the managing officers as to the regular and occasional appraisals of the performance and conduct of officers and employees and as to the use of the resulting ratings, plus the administrative procedures and devices used in implementing such prescriptions. Reliable and valid employee ratings are most needed for use in deciding upon promotions, demotions, transfers, and removals for cause; making upward and downward pay adjustments within the adopted graduated scales of pay; determining the order of layoff when the work forces must be reduced because of lack of work or funds; and evaluating the worth and effectiveness of the recruiting and selection procedures and devices.

EMPLOYMENT LIST: The names, usually arranged in the order of believed occupational success, of those who, as a result of employment tests and batteries of employment tests, are expected to be occupationally qualified and successful if appointed to a position in the class for which such tests are given. The term *employment list* is more descriptive and preferable to the widely used *register* and *eligible list*.

EMPLOYMENT TEST: Any set of procedures or any devices used to measure the extent to which one or more persons considered for employment possess the knowledge, skills, abilities, personal attributes, or other traits believed to be needed in performance of the position; and appraisals based upon work history.

EMPLOYMENT TESTS, BATTERY: A group of employment tests used to measure the extent to which one or more persons being considered for employment possesses the knowledge, skills, abilities, personal attributes, or other traits believed to be needed in the performance of the aggregate of tasks constituting a position that is to be filled. More often than not, a battery of tests rather than a single employment test is used in the selective process.

EMPLOYMENT TEST VALIDITY: The degree to which an employment test or a battery of employment tests actually predicts the occupational success of those considered for employment and appointed to a vacant position. The validity of most of the employment tests and batteries of employment tests in use today is largely unknown.

EMPLOYMENT TRAIT TEST: An employment test that is intended and constructed to discover the extent to which those considered for employment possess a single trait, or a group of closely related traits, believed to be significant in predicting occupational success. Among the employment trait tests are those that measure manual dexterity, the ability to use correct English, abstract intelligence, mechanical aptitude, and mechanical ability. Many but not all of the trait tests available for employment use have been carefully validated. Seldom does any one trait test predict occupational success, but many trait tests do screen out a high proportion of those lacking a needed trait.

FRINGE BENEFIT: Any work condition prescribed by the employer, either of his own volition or after negotiations with employees, that makes employment in the organization more attractive. Among the common fringe benefits are annual, sick, maternity, and military leaves, with or without pay or with reduced pay; retirement, unemployment, severance, and social security tax payments; coffee breaks; seniority, tenure, and reemployment rights; and shortening of the work hours without reduction in total pay. Often some "fringe benefits" are regarded as part of the pay of the officers and employees who receive them and sometimes a cash value is placed upon them in calculating total pay. They are better regarded, in the opinion of the writer, as work conditions, to be thought of in the same category as hours of work, or a part of the security program of the organization financed in whole or in part by the employer.

INDUCTION: The operation involved in making a new appointee to any position an understanding and productive worker as quickly as possible. As a rule the immediate superior of the newly appointed officer or employee acquaints him with the place of work; gives him work assignments; provides working space, tools and equipment; and explains work conditions and standards. In some cases, groups of new officers and employees are assembled for parts of the induction process.

IN-SERVICE TRAINING PLAN: The procedures and devices used in providing occupational in-service training of types considered desirable and feasible for the officers and employees of an organization, along with the prescriptions of the managing officers as to the conditions under which such training may be given and the time and manner of so doing. For the most part the immediate supervisor of a given officer or employee provides such training as a part of the day-to-day work, to the extent he considers it desirable and feasible. Sometimes groups of officers and employees may be assembled for formal in-service training work. In some cases, in some organizations, selected officers and employees are released from their regular tasks for stated periods to take approved courses in an educational or other institution.

LABOR TURNOVER: The extent to which changes in incumbents of positions occur in a given period of time, usually expressed in terms of the percentage of the number of changes to the total number of positions. The labor turnover in the whole organization or in specified subdivisions is useful in evaluating the success of the personnel management operations.

LAYOFF: The temporary separation of an officer or employee from his place in the organization because of lack of work or funds. Such separations may be for a short or long period and may become permanent; unless it becomes permanent the officer or employee who is laid off is normally restored to the position he held or to a similar one.

LEAVE: The approved absence of an officer or employee from work for a specified period. Leave may be taken with full or partial pay or without pay, because of mental or physical disability, or as one of the work conditions, to comply with legal requirements, or for any other reason. Annual, sick, maternity, military, and jury leaves are the commonest types for which leave with full pay is allowed.

LEAVE PLAN: The prescriptions of the managing officers about the kinds and amounts of leave that may be granted officers and employees and about the conditions under which such leave may be taken, plus the administrative procedures and devices used to implement such prescriptions.

MANAGING OFFICERS: The legislative body, the board of directors, the chief executive, the department heads, and others in a government or business organization who determine, direct, and normally participate in carrying on the operations of the organization. Some of the functions of the managing officers are to make final decisions as to the objectives and activities of the organization; to provide needed funds, physical plant, and facilities; to determine or pass upon the internal organization and the operating procedures; to determine the number and kind of positions to be authorized and established and their relationships, and to see that proper relationships among the operating units and with the public are established and maintained.

OCCUPATIONAL GROUP: The classes and incumbents of positions of a specific work type, usually of several levels, that are so much alike as to make possible similar treatment in carrying on personnel management operations.

ORIGINAL ENTRANCE: The selection and appointment of an officer or employee who at the time the selection and appointment operations are carried on is not an organization member.

PAY: The total remuneration of an officer or employee, made up of the cash payment plus the estimated or calculated value of any meals, lodging, laundry, uniform, medical and dental services, and other allowances provided. This definition of pay is substantially the same as that used for social security purposes. Because of the considerable variations in their meaning, the terms *salary, wages* and *compensation* are not used here. Travel allowances and payments are not included because they are properly reimbursement for expenses incurred rather than compensation. At times the cash value of the allowances provided is disregarded or intentionally underestimated as a means of paying more than the established rate; for the same reason, designated officers and employees are sometimes allowed to buy stock in the organization at less than the current market prices. Generally, however, the adopted rates of pay are intended to represent the total pay. Cash pay is determined by subtracting the value of allowances provided from such established rates. The various "fringe benefits" are not regarded herein as part of the pay.

PAY ADJUSTMENT: An upward or downward change in the total pay of an officer or employee, without change in his classification or major change in his duties, responsibilities, or organization relationships, within the adopted graduated scale of pay for his class of positions. The term is sometimes used with a different meaning, but in this book it is used only

115

with the meaning indicated. Downward pay adjustments within the adopted scale of pay for any class have been generally abandoned, but they may well become common again when and if reliable and valid employee ratings become widely available.

PAY PLANS: The end products of the processes used to produce the flat rates of pay and the graduated scales of pay for the classes of positions in an organization, plus the prescriptions of the managing officers as to their adoption, maintenance, amendment, and use. Pay plans are not yet used in all organizations and pay problems then are handled on the basis of precedents and improvisations.

PERSONNEL MACHINERY: The arrangements for achieving the personnel objectives, including the administrative devices that may be used in implementing the personnel program. The personnel machinery varies widely in different organizations and includes the central personnel agency, the personnel rules, and the personnel tools developed by the personnel technicians and the operating officers for use in implementing the personnel program.

PERSONNEL MANAGEMENT, ART OF: The methods and practices, based upon and derived from the science of personnel management, that when used give reasonable assurance of attaining desired personnel objectives.

PERSONNEL MANAGEMENT ASSIGNMENT: The specifications, in the personnel mandates, prescriptions, and authorizations and in the directives of the chief executive or others, of the roles of the chief executive, the department heads and their assistants, the individual officers and employees, the central personnel agency, or others in the implementation of the personnel program.

PERSONNEL MANAGEMENT, SCIENCE OF: The knowledge and experience that are of significance in carrying on personnel management operations in a government, business, or other organization having one or more employees in such a way as to aid in attaining stated personnel objectives.

PERSONNEL MANDATES, PRESCRIPTIONS, AND AUTHORIZATIONS: The formal and informal directives of the managing officers of an organization, specifying the scope and nature of the personnel program and the manner of carrying on the personnel management operations. The directives may be included in whole or in part in the constitution or charter of the organization, in enactments of the legislative body or the board of directors, in formal and informal pronouncements of the chief executive, in oral and written directives of the department heads to their subordinates, or in formally adopted personnel rules. In some organizations, both government and business, the personnel mandates, prescriptions, and authorizations are not covered by or included in any written documents or oral pronouncements. In nearly all large government organizations they are set forth in considerable detail in the constitution or charter, in the personnel legislation, or in the formally adopted personnel rules.

PERSONNEL OBJECTIVES: The personnel aims in any organization, as determined by the managing officers and by their authorized agents, to be attained or facilitated by means of the personnel management operations authorized and carried on therein.

PERSONNEL PROGRAM: The statement of the personnel objectives of the organization and the specifications of the machinery, devices, and procedures to be used in attainment of the objectives as indicated broadly in detail in the personnel mandates, prescriptions, and authorizations.

PERSONNEL RECORD PLAN: The system of records in any organization that shows the identity, department location, geographical location, title, pay, status, and employment history of the officers and employees therein; the significant facts and papers concerning the individual personnel transactions; and any additional information about personnel management operations that the managing and administrative officers consider necessary or desirable; plus the procedures and devices for establishing, maintaining and using such records.

PERSONNEL RULES: The prescriptions of the managing officers covering the development and adoption of the principal personnel tools, the manner of adopting, maintaining, and amending them, and their use in the handling of the personnel transactions.

PERSONNEL TECHNICIAN: A person well grounded in the science and the art of personnel management who, as the representative of the managing officers, the chief executive, or the central personnel agency of a government, business or other organization having employees, participates in technical personnel management operations. Often, in large organizations, there are different types of personnel technicians who give major attention to some particular phase of personnel technical work; for example, the classification and pay technician, and the employee rating technician.

PERSONNEL TOOL: Any device or procedure intended for use in handling the personnel transactions to attain desired personnel objectives with reasonable certainty. Some of the principal personnel tools are the positions classification plan, the pay plan, the recruiting plan, the employee rating plan, the separation plan, and the personnel record plan.

PERSONNEL TRANSACTION: Any operation or series of operations whose purpose is to establish, maintain, change or discontinue the employer-employee relationship. It includes any operation or series of operations relating to an established position, such as the original classification or the reclassification or the reallocation of a position.

PERSONNEL WORKING PRACTICES or FACTORS: Any one of the many rules accepted and used as an aid and guide in deciding upon a feasible course of personnel action that will be reasonably successful in attaining personnel objectives. These rules are based upon the appraisal of extensive, significant and representative data. A specific personnel governing practice is an aid and guide, not a pronouncement from which there may be no deviation as it relates to the personnel mandates, prescriptions, and authorizations; to the personnel program and assignment; to the personnel machinery; to the personnel tools; to the handling of the personnel transactions; or to any other type of personnel management operations.

POSITION: An aggregate of tasks performed by one person. A specific position may be permanent or temporary, year-round or seasonal, part time or full time. The aggregate of tasks constituting a position may be changed from time to time in view of changes in production needs, in internal organization, in operating procedures, and in the capabilities and interests of the incumbent. The changing, establishment, or discontinuance of any position is not part of the personnel management operations but belongs in the field of general management. In this book, the word *job* is not used as a synonym or substitute for the word *position* because it has a number of meanings that vary widely and often cannot be determined or even inferred from the context.

POSITION ALLOCATION: The process of determining and designating which individual positions are to be included in each of the recognized classes of positions. In this process, an individual position is usually identified by the organization unit in which it is located, by the existing title, and by the name of the present incumbent; any vacant position is labeled as such. In organizations where the individual positions are identified by some code symbol, that symbol is also used.

POSITION CLASSIFICATION: The grouping of all or designated positions in an organization, on the basis of their duties, responsibilities, organization relationships, and other significant characteristics, into homogeneous classes to be used as the basic personnel tool in carrying on the pay, recruiting, training and separation transactions. Position classification is a grouping of positions and not of employees.

POSITION CLASSIFICATION PLAN: The end product of the position classification process. The plan consists of the classes of positions recognized, each class identified by its title and its definition, the allocation of each of the individual positions to its appropriate class, and the prescriptions of the titles, and allocations. Complete and detailed class specifications or descriptions are not a part of the classification plan; their preparation is a separate operation, and the specifications are more accurately to be regarded as a supplementary product. The adopted rate or scale of pay for each person in the class is also not a part of the classification plan.

PREAUDIT AND CERTIFICATION OF PAYROLLS: The review of payrolls by the central personnel agency before payments for personal services are made and the certification, as a condition of making such payments, to the disbursing officers that

119

the items are in accordance with the personnel mandates and prescriptions of the managing officers. The preaudit and certification of payrolls seldom occurs in business or in small public organizations, but is usually a legal requirement in nearly all the public organizations that have a central personnel agency.

PROBATION APPOINTMENT: The placing by the appointing authority of a certified eligible in a vacant position for a trial or probation period to determine his probable occupational success. The length of the probation period is usually specified in the personnel laws or rules; it may vary in different organizations or for different classes of positions in the same organization. It is most frequently three, six, or sometimes twelve months.

PROMOTION: The moving of an officer or employee from one position to another at a higher level, as indicated by a higher flat or maximum rate of pay. A promotion, as thus defined, does not necessarily mean an immediate increase in the pay of the officer and employee promoted; there may be no change in pay when the graduated scales of pay for the two classes of positions overlap.

RECRUITING: The selection and appointment of any officer or employee brought into an organization from the outside or promoted, demoted, or transferred therein. Often the more formal term *recruitment* is used. The meaning of either term may be limited to the selective portion of the recruiting work, with the appointment designated by some such term as *placement* and with promotions, demotions, and transfers regarded as inservice personnel transactions rather than recruiting.

RECRUITING PLAN: The various devices and procedures used in the selection and appointment of those brought into the service of an organization and of those already in the organization who are promoted, demoted, and transferred therein, along with the prescriptions of the managing officers as to the use of such procedures and devices.

REMOVAL FOR CAUSE: The forced separation of an officer or employee from his position because of poor performance or unsatisfactory conduct. Such action may or may not include

120

the filing of charges and a hearing at which the administrative or other officers concerned present the reasons for the proposed removal and at which the officer or employee whose removal is sought is given the opportunity to answer the charges.

RESIGNATION: The action of an officer or employee who of his own volition permanently leaves his position.

RETIREMENT: The permanent separation of an officer or employee from the working force of an organization upon reaching a specified age or after a designated period of employment, with payments thereafter made to the retired officer or employee in accordance with the provisions of the retirement plan of the organization.

ROSTER CARD: The card on which are recorded the significant facts as to the employment history of one officer or employee. The roster card varies considerably in form and content from organization to organization, but usually includes the dates and the nature of any personnel transaction concerning the officer or employee, such as first employment, changes of status, pay adjustments, disciplinary actions, separations and, at times, additional data. The roster cards are useful as individual records and indispensible in the preaudit and certification of payrolls.

SAFETY PLAN: The prescriptions of the managing officers about the measures to be taken to assure, as far as possible, the protection of employees from accidents and injuries while on duty, and in some cases when going to and from work; aid in the treatment of such injuries while on duty; and the prevention of needless loss or damage to property, plus the administrative procedures and devices used to implement such prescriptions.

SCIENCE: A methodological activity, discipline or study comprising knowledge gained through repeated tests and experience. *See* PERSONNEL MANAGEMENT, SCIENCE OF

SECURITY PLAN: The prescriptions of the managing officers about the measures to be taken to assure officers and employees, as far as possible, of a high degree of security during their employment and after they leave the organization, plus the administrative procedures and devices used to implement such prescriptions. Among the common security devices are retirement and unemployment plans financed wholly or in part by the employer.

SEPARATION PLAN: The prescriptions of the managing officers about the measures to be taken to bring about separations from the organization of officers and employees who are no longer needed, who have reached the specified age of retirement, who have served in the organization for specified periods, or whose performance and conduct are such as to make their continued employment undesirable, plus the administrative procedures and devices used to implement such prescriptions. The term *separation plan* is a broad one that includes the various types of separations and the plans used for particular types of separations.

SUSPENSION: A disciplinary action that includes the temporary separation of an officer or employee from his position, without pay, due to unsatisfactory performance or conduct.

TECHNICIAN: A person who is well grounded in the science and art of a discipline and who consciously, consistently, and skillfully bases his actions upon this knowledge. *See* PERSONNEL TECHNICIAN

TEMPORARY APPOINTMENT: The placing by the appointing authority of some person, whose appointment may or may not be approved by the central personnel agency, in a vacant position for a limited period, usually because there is no employment list for the class of positions to which the vacant position has been allocated. In such cases the temporary appointment must be brought to an end after a certain period or when an employment list for the class is established. In other cases the temporary appointment is to a temporary position scheduled to continue for a few days, weeks, or months only.

TRANSFER: The moving of an officer or employee from one position to another that is allocated to a different class of the same level with the same flat or maximum rate of pay. A transfer does not usually involve an immediate change in the rate of pay.

1021500075P
Printed in the U.S.A.